STUDIES
IN THE BOOK OF
EZEKIEL

A quarter-shekel of Gaza Minoa from a unique specimen in the British Museum (much magnified). It was a silver coin struck on the Phoenician standard and dates from the latter part of the fifth century B.C. The obverse shows a bearded head wearing a crested Corinthian helmet with a bay-wreath upon it and is probably meant for Minos, the reputed founder of Gaza. The reverse—here represented—has the Hebrew Godhead figured as a bearded deity sitting on a winged and wheeled throne with a hawk on his outstretched hand. In the field beside him are the Aramaic letters *Y H W*, that is *Yahu*, the triliteral form of the name Jehovah. Confronting him is a mask-like face, probably that of the Egyptian god Bes (see p. 142 of text, iii (*b*)).

STUDIES
IN THE BOOK OF
EZEKIEL

BY THE REV.

JOHN BATTERSBY HARFORD

D.D. (CANTAB.)

CANON OF RIPON

CAMBRIDGE

AT THE UNIVERSITY PRESS

1935

CAMBRIDGE
UNIVERSITY PRESS

University Printing House, Cambridge CB2 8BS, United Kingdom

Published in the United States of America by Cambridge University Press, New York

Cambridge University Press is part of the University of Cambridge.

It furthers the University's mission by disseminating knowledge in the pursuit of
education, learning and research at the highest international levels of excellence.

www.cambridge.org
Information on this title: www.cambridge.org/9781107649460

© Cambridge University Press 1935

First published 1935
First paperback edition 2014

A catalogue record for this publication is available from the British Library

ISBN 978-1-107-64946-0 Paperback

CONTENTS

PREFACE

These Studies were to have been ushered into the world by a Foreword from Professor Burkitt, but owing to a grievous mischance that Foreword can now never be written. The University of Cambridge has been bereft of one of its brightest ornaments by his death and innumerable friends all over the world will lament his sudden passing. He was the kindest and most generous-hearted of friends, ever ready out of his great stores of learning to give help and encouragement to all who asked. He was good enough to refer to the present work as the only introduction to the modern critiques of Ezekiel, and it is as such an introduction that I have written the main part of this Exercise. It will, I trust, be found serviceable to all classes of Bible students. The two Excursuses, while addressed primarily to professional Bible critics, will, I hope, be found intelligible to all thoughtful readers. I must express my indebtedness to all the writers, whose words are commented on in these Studies, and to the friend at Marburg, who guided my early studies in German. I am also indebted to Dr A. B. Cook for showing me a replica of the coin which forms the Frontispiece, and for writing the inscription beneath it. Early versions of the Introduction and of Excursus II were delivered to the Easter Vacation School of the Bangor University College Faculty of Theology in March 1931 and to the Society for Old Testament Study in January 1933, and I venture to present this final result to the members of these two Bodies with respectful salutations.

J. BATTERSBY HARFORD

Ripon
30 May 1935

NOTE. The References are given as in the Hebrew Bible. Where the English version differs as to chapter and verse, the English reference is given in brackets.

CHAPTER I

CRITICISM UP TO A.D. 1900

There are two ways in which we may approach this Book. We may approach it from the divine side. From that point of view, we see it as a Holy Scripture, the essential purpose of which is to bring its readers face to face with God. As such, we use it in the inner prayer-room and in the pulpit, and no other Book gives us a more sublime vision of the Majesty of God.

But the Book has also a human side. If we approach it from that side, we see it as a literary work and, as such, it demands from us the same careful scholarly study of its phenomena that we should give to any worthy production of human workmanship. To use an analogy from Architecture, the study of the stones of a Cathedral may shew the student either that it has all been erected at one time by one generation of builders, as is the case at Salisbury, or that its present form is due to six different generations, as is the case at Ripon. In the latter case Saxon, early and late Norman, early, middle and late English men have all left outward and visible signs of the share that they took in the evolution of the Cathedral as it stands to-day. The value of the Sacred Building is in no way affected, except for good, by the reverent study of its architectural history. As with the Cathedral, so with the Book. The spiritual value of the Book, as a Holy Scripture, is in no wise affected, except for good, by the reverent study of its structure from what we may call its architectural side. To that we must now address ourselves. Its spiritual value will be dealt with in a final chapter.

We notice first the fact that the stones of which it is built, i.e. the Text or actual wording of it, is in certain parts exceptionally worn or dilapidated. The Masorites, the Jewish Editors of the Hebrew Text in the early Middle Ages, noted 166 variations in the margin of their MSS., but these only represent a small proportion, and these the least important, of the probable corruptions. A discriminating use of the Greek version provides us with many emendations, and the Syriac and Latin versions also lend their aid, but even then there remain a number of passages where conjectural emendation must be resorted to, if we are to arrive at an intelligible Text. Some of these passages we shall return to consider at a later stage.

But, dilapidated as its Text may be in parts, the main structure stands firm. If we may continue to use the analogy of a Cathedral, we must be struck on our first approach by the grandeur of its entrance portal. 'We find', writes Prof. Rudolf Otto of Marburg, 'the power of the Numinous, in its phase of the mysterious, to excite and intensify the imagination, displayed with particular vividness in Ezekiel.' The vision of the Almighty in the first chapter fills our mind, as we enter, with a profound sense of the Majesty of Him, who seeks to reveal His mind and will in this Book. And similar visions meet us in chapters viii to x and xl to xlii.

As we proceed up the nave of this literary Cathedral and take a rapid survey of the Building as it now stands, our next impression is that of symmetry. The Book falls naturally into two equal halves of twenty-four chapters each. The first half records (chapters i to iii) the call and commission of the prophet and (iv to xxiv) the prophecies of ruin, which were uttered before the destruction of Jerusalem in 586 B.C. In the second half we find, first, a collection of prophecies against foreign powers (xxv to xxxii) and of the destruction of Gog, Israel's final enemy (xxxviii–xxxix) and, between these, prophecies of the restoration and renewal of Israel (xxxiii–xxxvii), and finally we enter what we may call the chancel, nine chapters (xl–xlviii) which picture the worship and life of the restored community, partly in vision, partly in Temple laws.

Comparing the two halves, we are struck by the way in which the two answer to one another. Twice the prophet is brought in the power of the Spirit to Jerusalem and to the Temple. At his first visit (chapters viii–xi) he sees horrible idolatries carried on within the sacred enclosure of the first Temple and to his infinite sorrow he sees the glory of Jehovah leave the doomed Building and pass away to the East. At his second visit (xl–xliii) he sees a new Temple, which is separated from persons and things unholy, which is guarded by successive zones of ever greater holiness and which is built in perfect symmetry. In that Temple he sees, returning from the East, the glory of Jehovah. It fills the house, and he hears a voice, saying: 'I will dwell in the midst of the children of Israel for ever.'

We notice further that certain characteristic phrases run through the whole Book:

(1) 92 times the prophet is addressed as 'Son of man', a title which, as addressed to a prophet, only occurs once again in the Old Testament, viz. in Daniel (viii. 17);

(2) The divine title 'Lord Jehovah'* occurs 121 times in the introductory phrase: 'Thus saith Lord Jehovah', and

* Wherever in our English versions we find LORD or GOD printed in capitals, there in the Hebrew text we have the consonants of the sacred name JHVH. The word Jehovah is a hybrid word, the consonants of JHVH being read, not as originally pronounced, but with the vowels of Adonai, the Hebrew word for 'Lord'. For the last 2000 years 'Adonai' has been pronounced by the Jews in synagogue worship, wherever the sacred name occurs, to avoid possible profanation. The word 'Jehovah' is, however, a majestic word and it is familiar to us, not only by its use in our English Bible, but by its use in some of the finest hymns in our language. We do well therefore

(3) 81 times in the concluding formula: 'saith (lit. utterance of) Lord Jehovah', and in fifteen other passages, 217 times in all.

In the whole of the rest of the Old Testament the phrase 'Lord Jehovah' only occurs 78 times. In Jeremiah, for example, it occurs only 13 times, whereas 'saith Jehovah' without Lord occurs 158 times. The three phrases so far mentioned occur throughout the whole Book and may well be Editorial in character. But a very large number of other phrases occur over and over again in the body of the prophecies in the first thirty-nine chapters but are absent from the last nine:

(4) One very notable phrase, 'Ye shall know that I am Jehovah' (with occasional variations and additions) is used 74 times;

(5) 'the word of Jehovah came to me' occurs 49 times;

(6) 'I have spoken it' (with or without 'and I will do it') 49 times;

(7) 'as I live, saith Jehovah' 15 times (only 5 times elsewhere in the O.T.);

(8) 'I will scatter you among the nations and disperse you in the lands' 16 times;

(9) 'I will gather you from the peoples and will bring you in' 10 times;

(10) 'I will pour out my fury upon them (you)' 13 times;

(11) 'I lifted up my hand' (i.e. to swear an oath) 9 times;

(12) 'Because..., therefore...' 37 times (out of a total of 93 times in the O.T.).

These are but specimens of a large number of such recurrent phrases. There are also characteristic words, such as

(13) 'abominations' (used of idols) 43 times;

_____

to retain its use. For a full discussion of the use of the title 'Lord Jehovah' see Chapter x and Excursus ii.

(14) 'gillūlim' (a rare word for idols found elsewhere only in Lev. xxvi. 30, Deut. xxix. 16 (E.V. 17), 1 and 2 Kings (6 times) and Jer. l. 2), 39 times;

(15) נָשִׂיא (Nāsi) prince, occurring 37 times in seventeen chapters (20 times in xl to xlviii).

This last word is used by no other prophet, but in the Priestly Code and Priestly sections of Joshua it occurs 85 times (elsewhere only 9 times, in Kings, Chronicles and Ezra). [See Note on the Prince, pp. 65 f.]

It is not surprising, in view of the general symmetry and of the frequent recurrence of these characteristic phrases, that up to the end of the last century the great majority of writers regarded the whole Book as coming from one author and that author Ezekiel himself. 'No critical question arises', wrote Dr Driver in his Introduction to the Old Testament, 'in connection with the authorship of the Book; the whole from beginning to end bears unmistakably the stamp of a single mind', and again, 'the volume is methodically arranged, evidently by Ezekiel's own hand: his book in this respect forms a striking contrast to those of Isaiah and Jeremiah'. Cornill in 1891 spoke, if possible, even more decisively (but in later editions, 1905, etc., he spoke very differently). Smend said: 'One could not take out one section, without ruining the whole ensemble', and Bertholet, Kraetschmar and others in varying degrees gave utterance to the same opinion.

These writers were further all of one mind in regard to another very striking feature of the Book of Ezekiel. A study of its phraseology by Jewish Doctors of the Law long centuries ago had revealed the fact that in certain parts it presented a remarkable resemblance to the legal parts of the Pentateuch and especially to the Holiness Code (Lev. xvii to xxvi). We may note, for example, the thirty-three references to meal-, sin-, and trespass-offerings in Ezekiel xl to xlvi and the almost complete silence about them elsewhere.*

As examples of the very frequent use in chapters i to xxxix of phrases and constructions characteristic of Leviticus, we may take the following from Lev. i. 2: (a) 'When any man of you' (Hebrew construction 'a man when...', and so Lev. ii. 1, iv. 2, v. 1, 2, 4, 15, 17, vi. 1 (E.V. 2), vii. 21), so Ezek. xviii. 21 (lit. the wicked man when) and xxxiii. 2 (lit. a land when I bring) and nowhere else. (b) 'offereth', lit. bringeth near (Lev. and Num. 108 times in this sense), so Ezek. 7 times; rest of Old Testament 4 times. (c) An oblation (Korban, as Mark vii. 11). In Lev. i–vii 31 times, in the whole of P 77 times, so Ezek. xx. 28, xl. 43; nowhere else in the Old Testament.†

* 'meal-offering': Priestly Code 91 times; Ezek. 15; rest of Old Testament 13; total 119. 'sin-offering': P 92 times; Ezek. 14; 2 Chron., Ezra, Neh. 5; total 111. 'trespass-offering': P 28 times; Ezek. 4; rest 6 (including Isa. liii. 10); total 38. ('P' here and elsewhere = Priestly Code and Narrative.)

† See also the following:

Lev. ii. 1 'anyone' (Heb. 'soul'), so 36 times in Holiness Code and P; so Ezek. 4 times in xviii. 4, xxxiii. 6, elsewhere Deut. twice, Prov. once. Cf. 'souls' (pl.) = persons Holiness Code and P 7 times; so Ezek. 11 times, especially xiii. 18–20 8 times; elsewhere 3 times.

vii. 18 'shall bear their iniquity', so Ezek. iv. 4, 5, 6, xiv. 10.

xvii. 3 'whatsoever man there be' (Heb. 'man man', so Ezek. xiv. 4, same Heb.), 8, 10, 13 (4 times) 'of the house of Israel or of the strangers that sojourn {among them', in Israel'} so Ezek. xiv. 7.

10 'I will set my face against that soul...and will cut him off from among his people', so Ezek. xiv. 8.

7 'go a whoring' (after idols), so in Ezek. over 20 times.

xviii. 2, 4, 5, etc. 'I am Jehovah' (17 times) (+ your God) 21 times, so Ezek. xx. 5, 7, 19.

4 'my judgments shall ye do and my statutes shall ye keep',

These are but samples. In some chapters of Ezekiel, such as the eighteenth and the twentieth, almost every other phrase recalls a similar phrase in Leviticus. When Christian scholars began once more to study the Old Testament in the original Hebrew, they were at one with the Jewish Rabbins in explaining the resemblances as due to the fact that Ezekiel had so steeped himself in the study of the ancient law that it shaped all his thinking and coloured all his speech. But when modern historical methods of study came to be applied to the Old Testament, it became more and more difficult to maintain this position. Hardly a trace could be found in pre-exilic writings of any knowledge of the Levitical Law, and what apparent traces were found came to be suspected on good grounds as being patches made at a later time in the style which had by that time come to be in vogue. At last, between fifty and sixty years ago, a revolution of view took place. Ezekiel came to be regarded, not as the student resuscitating ancient law, but as, with others, the inaugurator of a new order of things. This order was based upon the older ritual usages, which had grown up during a long period at the Temple in Jerusalem, but it was, during the Exile and after, systematized and developed to form a compact body of law, which would form a hedge round the Chosen People. Wellhausen called Ezekiel 'the priest in the prophet's mantle', and looked upon him as 'the connecting link between the prophets and the

---

so Ezek. xx. 19.   5 'which if a man do, he shall live in them', so Ezek. xx. 21.   6 'uncover nakedness' (and 19 times), so Ezek. xxii. 10 and 4 times (elsewhere once).

ix. 6, 23 + 10 times in P 'The glory of Jehovah', so Ezek. i. 28 and 9 times; and 'the glory of the God of Israel', so Ezek. viii. 4 and 4 times.

xxvi. 22–26 'I will send the beast of the field...destroy your cattle', etc., etc., so Ezek. iv. 16, v. 16, 17, vi. 3, xiv. 13, 15, 17, 19, 21.

8   STUDIES IN THE BOOK OF EZEKIEL

law'. Ezekiel, he said, 'claims to be a Prophet and starts
from prophetic ideas, but they are not his own ideas; they are'
inherited from his predecessors and especially from Jeremiah.
'He is by nature a priest and his peculiar merit is that he
enclosed the soul of prophecy in the body of a Community,
which' centred not round a king, but round a Temple and
its worship. 'Chapters xl to xlviii are the most important in
his book and have been called, not incorrectly, the key of the
Old Testament.' This view of the Book and of its influence
upon subsequent Jewish history has long been dominant in
this country and abroad.

Chapter II

FROM 1900 TO HERRMANN

In certain respects, however, both the opinions just referred to, viz. the unity of authorship and the relation of the author to the Law, have not gone unchallenged in recent years. As regards the first point, we must remember that this Book is not an isolated phenomenon. It is one of a whole series of prophetical Books and, if we approach it after a previous study of Isaiah or Jeremiah, we cannot but be prepared to admit that this Book also may have come to us, not entirely as it originally took shape under the hands of him whose name it bears, but rather as it took shape under the hands of an Editor or Editors who finally put it together. This latter is the view which has emerged in the last thirty years. A more thorough analysis of the Book has seemed to shew the existence in it of certain secondary elements.

KRAETSCHMAR (1900) was so impressed by the number of 'duplications' (i.e. of passages which seemed to say the same thing a second time) that he propounded the theory that, out of original Ezekielian material, two independent recensions had been made, which were afterwards put together to form our present Book.

JAHN (1905), however, denied that there were two recensions. He thought that later scribes had written in the margin revised versions of many passages which adapted the prophetic messages to the ideas and needs of the later generation, and that then still later copyists inserted these marginal versions into the Text.

HERRMANN, a devout and reverent scholar, now Professor

at Münster, in 1908 published *Ezechiel-Studien* and in 1924 a full Commentary on the Book in Sellin's series. In these he, like Jahn, rejects the idea of two recensions, but he considers Jahn to be far too prone to see 'later views' where they do not exist. At the same time he does recognize in a number of passages the intrusion of stranger hands. Let us look at three of these passages.

Chapter xii. Five times over (verses 1, 8, 17, 21, 26) comes the introductory phrase, 'the word of Jehovah came unto me, saying'. The last two paragraphs have little or no connection with those that precede. In verses 1–6 the description of the symbolic actions—putting together (lit.) 'articles of exile', digging through the wall, carrying out the bundle ('by day', verse 4, but according to verse 6, 'in the dark') with his face covered—is in such a state of confusion that we are compelled to see the intrusion of another hand. Note the repetition of 'before their eyes' six times in three verses and other signs of duplication. Note also the use of the word 'prince' of the king in verses 10 and 12. These verses are almost certainly an explanation added at a later time.

Chapters iii. 16–21 and xxxiii. 1–9. Here we have an example of duplication. Both passages set forth the prophet's task as that of a watchman. The latter passage seems to have been the original, because there, in the following section (verses 10–20), we can see how the conception of his task as that of a watchman arose. At the same time Herrmann suggests that Ezekiel may himself, at a later time, have inserted the earlier passage in its present position, because he realized now that what he had later seen to be the nature of his task had really been its nature from the beginning.

Chapter xx. 32–44. In verse 1 we read that certain elders came to enquire of Jehovah, and they are met (verse 3) by the emphatic reply: 'As I live, saith Lord Jehovah, I will not be enquired of by you.' This is followed (verses 4–30) by a review of the past relations between Jehovah and His people, which is redolent of phrases that occur in Lev. xxvi and which is closed in verse 31 by a repetition of Jehovah's emphatic refusal to be enquired of by such a people. The following section (verses 33–44) presents a quite new theme. The utterance of the exiles (verse 32) could not have arisen out of the occasion set forth in verses 1–31. It seems to have arisen out of an unqualified prophecy of ruin, to which the people in effect reply: 'Very well; if there is no hope that Jehovah will deliver us, then we will simply give up His worship and will serve the same gods of wood and stone as the nations around us.' The prophet counters this evil proposal by an encouraging prediction that Jehovah will bring them once more into the wilderness, cleanse them from their pollutions and lead them back to serve Him in their own holy mountain. This later prophecy, says Herrmann, may have been attached to the earlier, in order to soften its harshness, at a time when the predicted destruction of Jerusalem had taken place, and when the need was to revive hope.

These and numerous other passages, especially some in chapters xl–xlviii, as reviewed by Herrmann, do seem to justify him in arriving at the following conclusion. Whereas some earlier scholars had pronounced the Book to be the result of a sustained literary effort made at one time, from which no part could be removed without disarranging the whole, Herrmann would have us see a Book which bears all the marks of being a collection of minor independent utterances spoken on different occasions and put together many years later, just as were the Books of Isaiah and Jeremiah. The dates prefixed to various sections may indicate an intended chronological ordering of the whole, but the oracles standing in the Book between two dated passages were not necessarily spoken in the period between them. Each oracle must be separately studied and its period judged by its contents. At the same time Herrmann holds on to the belief that in the main the Book is by Ezekiel himself. He pictures Ezekiel in his later life as putting together his earlier utterances, working for a long time at it, editing and correcting and enlarging as new circumstances demanded. The reference to the fate of Zedekiah in chapter xii. 12 would come under this last head. Herrmann points to chapter xiv. 1–11, where we seem to have two speeches, delivered by Ezekiel at different times (note the formula in verses 4 and 6). Here, he says, we have an interesting example of Ezekiel's literary method. As one who cares for souls, as a practising pastor, it does not seem at all difficult to Ezekiel to say the same thing twice, when he can elucidate it helpfully in different ways. Repetitions, which may seem to us tedious at first sight, assume a different aspect when we realize that they are the outcome of a preacher's life work. The Book, however, is not a volume of sermons chronologically arranged in order of delivery, but rather a collection of sermon-notes, which had, as a rule, no definite statement as to time and place attached to them. These were at a later time compiled and arranged by Ezekiel himself, but also added to by later hands, with a view to immediate edification. If we do not agree to this, then, says Herrmann, the only alternative is to abandon a whole number of passages as non-Ezekielian. If we do agree to it, then we may regard certain inconsistencies between adjacent passages as having been introduced by Ezekiel himself towards the end of his life. But even then, Herrmann says, we are obliged to recognize that there remain certain passages, especially in chapters xliii–xlviii, where this explanation is insufficient.

Chapter III

HÖLSCHER

But now, can Herrmann's solution be unreservedly accepted? In two directions serious objections have been raised.

Gustav Hölscher in 1924 (at that time Professor at Marburg but now at Bonn) published a fresh investigation, entitled *Hesekiel, der Dichter und das Buch* (Ezekiel, the Poet and the Book). Previous writers had questioned the ascription of the whole Book to Ezekiel, but had obtained no hearing. Hölscher's vigorous handling of the problem compelled attention. 'Ezekiel', he said, 'has been one of the most misunderstood men of Hebrew literature.' 'Here (in this Book) are two different worlds', that of Ezekiel and that of a later Editor or Editors. Duhm in his Commentary on Jeremiah reduced that prophet's own work to sixty short pieces, amounting in all to about 250 verses. And now Hölscher cries: 'What Duhm did for Jeremiah, I do for Ezekiel.' Both prophets were of the old school; they cast their prophecies into poetic form. In our present Book we see, on the one hand, accounts in the first person of visions and of divine pressure upon the prophet together with a series of fine dramatic poems, which portray the evils about to fall upon Jerusalem and her allies, Tyre and Egypt, and, on the other hand, a number of prosaic discourses, full of borrowed and conventional phrases, occurring over and over again, which first denounce the iniquities of the house of Israel and then, later, promise restoration and renewal. Only the first of these two series is the genuine Ezekiel. He was a Poet, not a Legalist. The literary connections with the Levitical

Law and with the Book of Jeremiah have nothing to do with him. They are due to the later Editor, who lived near the time of Nehemiah. This man came into the possession of the genuine Ezekielian material and felt that, by judicious working over and supplementing, the ancient prophet might be made to speak effectively to the men of the later generation. So far from the compilers of the Levitical Law having derived their inspiration from the Ezekiel of the early years of the Exile, it is they who influenced the later Editor. He assumed that these laws had been binding upon the Israel of Ezekiel's time and arraigned the people accordingly for their breaches of it. As a matter of fact the genuine Ezekiel shews no prejudice against foreign ideas. He borrows from Babylonia the ideas of the Garden of God and the Mountain of God in the North and of the expulsion of primitive man from the Garden (xxxi. 8 and xxviii. 14–16). He has no prophecy against Babylon. On the contrary he, like Jeremiah, is pro-Babylonian, and he sets himself against the policy of the nationalist dreamers, who thought to win freedom from Babylon by alliances with Egypt and Tyre. The later Editor took up the same attitude against Egypt and Tyre, but he betrays his later date by shewing, e.g. his knowledge of the overthrow of the Egyptian power by Cambyses in 525 B.C. He also seems to assume (xx. 40 ff.) the rebuilding of the Temple under Zerubbabel in 515 B.C., for he records the promise: 'In my holy mountain all the house of Israel shall serve me; there will I require your offerings and...oblations...', but does not deem it necessary to include a promise that the Temple shall be rebuilt. Accordingly Hölscher would date the first editing of the Book between 500 and 450 B.C.

This drastic handling of the Book, which leaves to Ezekiel himself only about 143 verses out of 1272, startling as it is, presents itself in an attractive guise in two respects:

(i) The very title of Hölscher's treatise: 'The Poet and the Book', brings out an element in the Book of Ezekiel which we have not hitherto noticed, namely its poetic quality. Hölscher prints fifteen passages as poems: iv. 1–2, 9–11 The siege of Jerusalem, symbolized by an engraved tile and rationed food. v. 1–2 Hair shaved off and burnt, cut and scattered. xv. 2–5 The useless vine, burnt to the ground. xvi. 3–12, 15, 24f. The outcast infant, adopted and brought up, but unfaithful. xvii. 3–9 The two eagles and the vine shoot. xix. 2–9 The lioness and her two whelps. xxi. 9–11, 14–16 The song of the sword. xxiii. 12–27 (less glosses) The two sisters, wedded but wanton. xxiv. 3–5, 16f. The boiling pot and its contents. These nine all refer to Jerusalem. The remaining six refer to Tyre and to Egypt. xxvii. 3b–9a, 25–36 Tyre as a beautiful ship, wrecked at sea. xxviii. 12b–19 The prince of Tyre. xxix. 3b–5a The dragon, i.e. the crocodile, of Egypt. xxxi. 3–4a, 6–8 The great pine-tree. xxxii. 2 The Nile-monster (a fragment). xxxii. 18–27 (parts) Lamentation over Egypt in Sheol.

These poems, rescued by Hölscher with much difficulty from manifold excrescences and, as a result, problematical in detail at the best, are ascribed by him to Ezekiel, together with the introductory narrative of the appearance of the storm cloud from the North (i. 4), the giving and eating of the roll and the commission to proclaim the message written therein, the return to Tel-abib and the seven days' astonished silence (i. 28f., ii. 8–10, iii. 2, 10–12, 14–16, 24b) and the greater part of chapters viii and ix.

(ii) On the other hand Hölscher claims that by his analysis he has cleared Ezekiel from the charge of diffuseness and commonplaceness, which are so frequently brought against him. If we may use of Ezekiel words which Prof. Peake used of the Book of Jeremiah: 'the style is often diffuse and pedestrian; it abounds in stereotyped formulae and constant repetitions and draws not a little from earlier writers', then, if Hölscher can prove his thesis that these elements are not from Ezekiel's pen but from those of his Editors, has he not conferred a benefit upon us?

But, while we recognize that Hölscher's picture of the Poet-preacher would have its attractive side, if it could be proved, yet we may both question whether the analysis is sound, and also feel that the process which professes to cut out the diffuse and pedestrian has also cut out some of the finest parts of the Book, such as the visions of the resurrection of the dry bones in chapter xxxvi and of the river of the water of life in chapter xlvii.

(i) The first question which arises out of Hölscher's argument is this: Was prophecy in the days of Jeremiah and Ezekiel couched always, and only, in poetic form? Hölscher answers 'Yes'. But the general verdict is to the contrary. George Adam Smith, in his chapter on 'The Poet' in his Baird Lecture on Jeremiah (1922), shews convincingly that, while there is much in the remains of the ancient Hebrew prophets which is genuine poetry—of its kind—yet these passages of poetry 'issue from and run into contents of prose unmistakable'. We cannot now trace the exact border between poetry and prose, because the text is frequently uncertain and because the prose has often a rhythm approximating to metre, but few critics accept the results set forth by Duhm in the case of Jeremiah, and Hölscher's attempts to produce similar results for Ezekiel have fared no better.

Taking first the passages which are claimed as poems, it is difficult to see real poems in the scraps about the tile in chapter iv and the hair in chapter v, which are all that survive the surgical operations performed by Hölscher's critical knife

in these chapters.* Here and in the subsequent passages the
appearance of poetry is only arrived at by the elimination of
extremely numerous supposed glosses and additions. And if,
as the hypothesis requires, the later Editor came into the
possession of the Ezekielian poems at a subsequent date, it is
also difficult to understand why he should have treated them
with such slight regard for their poetic form as to make it
almost impossible to recover their original shape. Hölscher
himself frankly and expressly emphasizes (p. 90) that his

* Here is the first so-called poem, the words omitted by Hölscher
being put in square brackets:

    iv. 1 [Thou also, Son of man]
        Take thee a tile
        And lay it before thee
        [and] Portray upon it a city
        [Even Jerusalem]
      2 [and] Lay siege against it
        [and thou shalt] Build against it a Tower
        [and] Cast up against it a mound
        [and] Set camps against it
        [and] Plant battering rams against it round about
        [omit verses 3 to 8]
      9 [And thou] Take to thee wheat and barley
        [and] Bean [and] lentils [and] millet [and] spelt
        [and] Put them in one vessel
        And make thee bread thereof
        [omit rest of verse]
     10 [and thy meat which thou shalt] Eat
        [shall be by weight] (only) twenty shekels a day
        From time to time [shalt thou] eat it
     11 [and thou shalt] Drink water [by measure] the sixth part
          of a hin.
        From time to time [shalt thou] drink it.

In chapter v the following words are cut out:
v. 1 [And thou, son of man...take thee a barber's razor and...
2 in the midst of the city...and thou shalt take...and about it
and...thou shalt...and I will draw out a sword after them.]

'renderings cannot claim to be exact, not only because in many details the extraction of the genuine stock of these poems and the establishing of their original text necessarily remains and must remain quite uncertain, but also because as regards Hebrew metre we are still far from being able to establish definite laws. The translations are meant only to set forth the result of the analysis in rough outlines.' Hölscher claims that, in spite of this, the general distinction between the really metrical and the purely prosaic can be pretty certainly preserved and that passages which are badly corrupt and especially complicated are as a rule genuine, while the passages which are textually in much better condition and which from the literary point of view are more simple are the work of the first Editor and of more recent supplementers. But with every desire to study the phenomena without bias of any kind, it seems impossible to accept Hölscher's results as satisfactory. It is easy to see the temptation that it must have been to him to find poetry at all costs in those passages which on grounds of phraseology or outlook he would wish to recognize as Ezekielian, and on the other hand to fail to see poetry in other passages which on similar grounds seem to him to be secondary. Even as regards these grounds Hölscher is not really consistent in the applications of his own methods. If for example we look at his treatment of chapter xix. 1–9 we see that according to his own theory the words 'to the land of Egypt' should have been struck out as mixing fact with picture after the manner of the Editor but they are retained for the sake of the Hebrew metre, while on the other hand in verse 9 'to the king of Babylon' and 'on the mountains of Israel' are struck out as Editorial, although here also the metre demands their retention. Again, according to Hölscher, the poem, shorn of its present (Editorial?) introduction in verse 1, begins: 'Thy mother was a lioness', and this is regarded as genuine and intelligible, but the beginning of the corresponding poem (verse 10): 'Thy mother was as a vine', is rejected as unintelligible for lack of introduction and is therefore to be regarded as a secondary appendix. It is interesting to compare Hölscher's 'poems' with the passages which are treated as poems in Moffatt's Translation of the Old Testament. Moffatt agrees with Hölscher in seeing poems in six chapters, but in seven others he sees none, where Hölscher sees them, and in six others he sees poems where Hölscher does not.

(ii) When we turn from the poetical to the prose prophecies, we are conscious of a distinct change of atmosphere and colouring at certain points. In some passages there is a distinct plethora of stock phrases and of Levitical language and (in certain cases) of Aramaic colouring, which seem to justify their attribution either with Hölscher to a later Editorial hand or at best with Herrmann to Ezekiel in his old age.

(iii) There remains the argument that certain events, such as Cambyses' conquest of Egypt in 525 B.C., seem to be known to the writer and therefore the passages which shew such knowledge must be prophecies after the event. The cogency of such argument for us depends upon our view of prophecy in general. To those who believe that prophetic souls were given to see, dimly but yet really, in ways denied to ordinary men, events which cast their shadows before, such a priori arguments are quite unconvincing.

To sum up our discussion so far, Herrmann and Hölscher, so far as analysis is concerned, are not so far apart. Both are agreed that these prophecies have been freely glossed and that younger supplementers have added whole paragraphs and sections to the work. The difference between them lies in this, that Herrmann would retain as Ezekiel's the main bulk of the prose prophecies and explain the varied tone and outlook and phraseology as shewing that Ezekiel worked over his prophecies

2-2

in his old age, altering and supplementing from time to time without meticulous regard to consistency, while Hölscher would transfer them bodily to the credit of the Editor (or Editors), who in his view wrote them at least 100 to 150 years later and to whom in the main is due the order and symmetry of the whole.

In regard to the last nine chapters of the Book, which we have called the choir of this literary Cathedral, both men agree that they form a complicated structure, which has only attained its present shape as the result of a gradual compilation. Both find the clue to the original intention in xl. 4 and xliv. 5. Both recognize chapters xl–xlii and xliv. 4–19 as falling within the scheme thus outlined and regard the greater part of the residue as due to later hands, but as before Herrmann assigns the earlier nuclei to Ezekiel, while Hölscher assigns them to the principal Editor. The problems raised by these nine chapters are too large to be discussed at this stage. They will be dealt with separately in Chapter ix.

CHAPTER IV

TORREY, SMITH, HERNTRICH

We stated at the commencement of Chapter II, that in two directions Herrmann's solution of the Ezekielian problem has been met by serious objections. In that chapter we dealt with the objections and with the counter theory of Prof. Hölscher. In this chapter counter theories of a different kind will be set forth.

I. In 1930 C. C. Torrey, Professor of Oriental Languages in Yale University, U.S.A., published a book, entitled *Pseudo-Ezekiel and the Original prophecy*.* For the last twenty years Torrey has sought to prove that the whole story of a Babylonian Exile and Return is pure fiction. The Book of Ezekiel, as it stands, blocks the way. He must therefore shew that the author never lived in Babylonia and that all the prophecies have their scene in Judah and Jerusalem. In the same way he has sought to shew that 'Second Isaiah' also had originally nothing to do with a Babylonian Exile and that the five references to Cyrus and to Babylon and Chaldaea are due to a later Editor and must be excised. Further, Jeremiah seems to recognize the Exile, but, says Torrey, in its present form it is a book which has been extensively doctored in the third century B.C. in order to bring it into line with the same scheme.

But what possible object can any body of men have had in effecting such radical transformations? Torrey's answer is that in the third century B.C. an internecine struggle was going on between the Samaritans and the Jews. The two bodies had finally split. The Samaritans had set up a rival Temple on the ancient sacred site at Shechem. They had their sacred copy

* Yale University Press, New Haven, Connecticut.

of the Law. They claimed that they, and not the Judaeans, had retained unimpaired the genuine ancient tradition, whereas Jerusalem had been destroyed, its Temple burnt, its priests dispersed and the true tradition lost. The Jews found it hard to refute this theory, but at last they hit upon an ingenious plan. They invented the Babylonian Exile. A body of Jews with priests at their head, they said, had been deported to Babylonia. There the best of them had preserved the Law and the old traditions and had returned to the land of Judah, bringing their precious records with them. The land meantime had lain derelict and uninhabited for seventy years, keeping her Sabbaths, as foreshadowed in Lev. xxvi. 34, 35. The returned exiles restored everything as it had been before. In the third century B.C., 300 years after the destruction of Jerusalem, all this could be asserted and no one could prove the contrary. The Book of Chronicles-Ezra-Nehemiah was written at this time, and built up its version of the history of Israel on this theory so successfully that, at least as regards the Persian period, for which it is the sole historical authority, it has been accepted both by Jews and Christians as genuine history. But as a matter of fact, Torrey says, the real course of events was quite different. According to Jer. lii. 28–30 only a small number of high-class Jews were taken to Babylonia with their king. The remainder fled to Edom, Moab, Ammon and neighbouring lands and returned again as soon as the coast was clear (Jer. xl. 11–12). The figures in 2 Kings xxiv. 14–16 and xxv. 11 are much exaggerated. The land was doubtless soon repopulated. The idea of its lying uninhabited for seventy years is quite incredible (in spite of 2 Chron. xxxvi. 2; cf. Lev. xxvi. 34f.).

This digression has been necessary in order to put in clear light the framework into which Torrey seeks to place the Book of Ezekiel. His argument is as follows:

1. 'Everywhere with rare exceptions we see the handiwork of one man.' 'Certain strongly marked literary characteristics run through the whole work from the first chapter to the last.' 'The great prophecy belongs to the prophet, who speaks throughout in the first person. The same peculiar style and diction appears in every chapter, the flavour of the poetry is exactly that of the prose.'

2. At the same time the handiwork of an Editor is also to be discerned. For example, take chapter i. 1–4:

(a) The first and the fourth verses are written in the first person, but between them come two verses in the third person. The original author could not have so written.

(b) In verse 1 reference is made to 'the thirtieth year', but no indication is given as to the era of which it was the thirtieth year. Endless fruitless conjectures have been made, but it is 'sun-clear', as soon as the solution is pointed out. 'The thirtieth year' can only be the thirtieth year of the reign of a king. One later king of Judah did reign for thirty years and more—viz. Manasseh. Evidently the original author professed to have received his call in the reign of king Manasseh. The words 'which was the fifth year of king Jehoiachin's captivity were added by a later hand with the express purpose of transferring the Book into the time of the Captivity and into Babylonia. The same hand altered the year-datings—thirteen in all—which are scattered through the Book and which end in xl. 1, and added a very few other passages—some sixteen in all—which describe the author as dwelling in the midst of the exiles in Babylonia, or as being transported by the Spirit to and from Jerusalem.

3. In chapter after chapter the prophecies are addressed not to exiles, among whom he is supposed to be living, but to the inhabitants of Judaea and Jerusalem. He is told not to write, but to 'speak' (iii. 4, 11, xxxiii. 2, etc.) Jehovah's words. His hearers are to be 'the children of Israel' (10 times), 'the

house of Israel' (81), 'the people of the land' (9), 'the rebellious house' (13), 'the children of thy people' (1). The first series of speeches (chapters iv to vii) are addressed to Jerusalem, the mountains of Israel, the land of Israel. By divine command he performs symbolic acts (chapter iv, etc.) and in v. 2 it is expressly ordered that he shall burn the hair 'in the midst of the city'. In chapter xii he performs another series of actions, symbolizing how the people of Jerusalem, with their prince at their head, would go into exile. All these actions could only be of value, if done in the actual sight of the people, for whose warning they were performed. The 'second person' in verse 20, 'and *ye* shall know...', makes it clear that in verse 19 also the verbs were originally in the second person, in harmony with the initial words: 'Say unto the people of the land', and that they have been altered to the third person to make it appear that they were spoken to the exiles. In chapter xi Ezekiel, being transported by the Spirit to the east gate of the Temple, sees Pelatiah and twenty-four other men standing there and is told to prophesy against them. He does so and in verse 13 we read: 'And it came to pass, when I prophesied, that Pelatiah died. *Then* fell I down upon my face and cried... and said: Ah, Lord Jehovah, wilt thou make a full end of the remnant of Israel?' Apart from verses 1 and 24, which speak of his seeing this in vision, while he was in Tel-abib, everyone would regard this as happening in Jerusalem. Once more, in chapter xxiv, the prophet is ordered to use the symbol of the boiling pot, and when 'the delight of his eyes' is taken from him, he is to wear no mourning, and verse 24 says: 'Thus Ezekiel shall be unto you a sign; according to all that he hath done, shall ye do, and when this cometh, ye shall know that I am Lord Jehovah.' These words seem only intelligible, if the sign was done in the sight of the inhabitants of Jerusalem. These are but samples of phenomena, which occur in one chapter after another and which seem to compel us to believe that the prophet spoke and acted in Judaea and not in Babylonia.

4. The sins which are condemned are the very sins which are spoken of in 2 Kings xxi. 2–7 and 16 as prevailing during the reign of king Manasseh: worship in high places, altars to Baal, Asherahs, worship of the host of heaven in the very courts of the Temple, Moloch worship by the sacrifice of young children in the fire, the practice of augury and the shedding of much blood in Jerusalem. According to 2 Kings xxiii these evils were rooted out by Josiah and their recurrence made impossible by burning dead men's bones upon the altars, defiling Topheth, burning the Asherah and the chariots of the sun and putting down wizardry. Jehoiakim might be a godless king but 2 Kings xxiii–xxiv gives not even a hint that the iniquities of the time of Manasseh were reintroduced. On the contrary xxiii. 26 and xxiv. 3 affirm that the final overthrow of the Kingdom of Judah was due, not to a return to idolatry on the part of the generation then living, but to 'the sins of Manasseh and the innocent blood that he shed and Jehovah would not pardon'. Yet according to the traditional dates of Ezekiel's prophecies and of certain prophecies of Jeremiah said to be spoken in the days of Jehoiakim, all the worst forms of forbidden worship were in full operation within one year after the death of Josiah and continued until the fall of the city (Ezek. viii, etc.). Could this possibly have happened? Torrey answers: 'No.' The destruction and pollution of the high places under Josiah were radical and the book of the Law was not lost again. 2 Kings must be relied upon, and Jeremiah and Ezekiel, when correctly interpreted, do not contradict it. The passages in Jeremiah, which denounce the practice of Moloch worship, were all spoken before the reformation under Josiah, and the passages in Ezekiel were put by the original author into the mouth of a supposed prophet in the

days of Manasseh. They were only afterwards brought down to the exile of Jehoiachin.

5. 'Ezekiel' never refers to his contemporary Jeremiah and even records the declaration of Jehovah (xxii. 30) that He sought for a man to stand in the gap and found none. The reason is that the prophecy is true to its (supposed) historic setting in the reign of Manasseh.

[6 to 9 are arguments to prove that the original Book must be dated actually in the third century B.C.]

6. The reference to Persians (xxvii. 10 and xxxviii. 5) in the armies of Tyre and of Gog, and two passages which seem to shew a knowledge of Alexander the Great (xxvi. 10 the conqueror of Tyre entering in with chariots and wagons—a feat only possible when Alexander built a great mole from the mainland in 332 B.C.). The words 'Nebuchadrezzar, king of Babylon' are a later insertion. Note their strange position. In chapters xxxviii–xxxix Gog is plainly Alexander and 'Magog and the isles' are the Macedonian Kingdom and the Grecian coastlands (see Gen. x. 2).

7. The Hebrew of Ezekiel is coloured by Aramaic usages, only paralleled in Daniel, Esther and Ecclesiastes.

8. The author of Ezekiel by his use of Levitical language, of phrases of Second Isaiah, of secondary parts of Jeremiah and of the first half of Daniel shews his knowledge of these Books, and the first certain evidence of the existence of his Book is Ecclesiasticus (xlix. 8), which was written about 180 B.C.

9. 'The oldest Jewish tradition recognizes no Babylonian prophet.' The Talmudic treatise, Baba Bathra, states that 'the men of the great synagogue wrote Ezekiel, the Twelve, Daniel and Esther'.

From all this Torrey draws the conclusions (1) that a man, probably of priestly rank, living in Jerusalem in the third century B.C., on the basis of 2 Kings xxi. 10, put into the mouth of a prophet in Manasseh's days passionate warnings and then reminded his readers how, when these warnings were disregarded, the punishment fell; (2) that some thirty years later an Editor, in the interest of the new theory of Babylonian Exile and Return, altered the Book so successfully by transferring its prophecies to a very different time and place, that for 2000 years no one perceived that anything was wrong.

Professor Torrey's theory is a novel and revolutionary one. It must, like all others, be judged according to the evidence adduced. But before doing so, we must take note of two other explanations of the Book, which have appeared in recent years and which, in spite of great differences, agree in one important point, viz. the place where, and the people to whom, the main prophecies of the Book were delivered.

II. Dr James Smith in 1931 published *The Book of the Prophet Ezekiel, a new Interpretation.** His book was in the press before Dr Torrey's work was published and is therefore a quite independent study of the Ezekielian problem. It is therefore the more striking that he has come to a similar conclusion in two respects, viz. (1) that Ezekiel's prophecies are addressed to the people of Palestine and appear to belong to the time of Manasseh, and (2) that they were actually spoken in Palestine and not in Babylonia. Where he differs from Torrey is that he believes that these prophecies are genuine speeches of a man of God, who really lived and worked in the days of Manasseh, and that he was a North Israelite, speaking to his own countrymen from some place in North Israel and to North Israelite exiles.

In justification of these latter views, Dr James Smith points to the frequent use of the phrase 'house of Israel' and sets a special meaning upon it; he seeks to account for the peculiarities of diction throughout the Book as due to the extent to

* Published by the S.P.C.K.

which the speech of North Israelites had been coloured by the influence of the foreign element which ever since the taking of Samaria had dwelt amongst them. He argues on the same lines as Torrey, but quite independently, that there are no signs of a pagan reaction under Jehoiakim and Zedekiah, and that therefore the depraved Temple worship in chapter viii must be pre-Josianic and belong to the reign of Manasseh. He interprets 'our captivity' (xxxiii. 21) as beginning in the year 734 B.C., the year in which the king of Assyria deported the populations of Naphtali and Dan, and therefore 'the twelfth year of our captivity' as being the year 722 B.C. in which Samaria was smitten, and 'out of Jerusalem' as one of the insertions made by an Editor. Dr James Smith, like most critics of late years, has to resort to an Editor in order to explain the passages which speak of a Babylonian environment. This Editor was a Judaean and seeks to conceal the fact that the prophet belonged to the despised North, and that the Fall of the City referred to in xxxiii. 21 was that of Samaria and not of Jerusalem, by transferring the whole prophecy to the exile of Jehoiachin. The date given in chapter xl. 1 is the year 709–8 B.C. and Ezekiel may have contemplated (at a time when many of the high places were rebuilt, see xvii. 27–32) a new Temple on 'the mountain of the height of Israel', while the Temple at Jerusalem still stood intact. The whole theory is ingeniously worked out. The discussion of it must, however, be reserved until one further theory is set forth.

III. The latest interpretation of the Book of Ezekiel was published in 1932 by Volkmar Herntrich of the University of Kiel, entitled *Ezechielprobleme*. His aim is to base upon a detailed analysis of the Text an answer to the question: What is the historical situation of the Prophet? He largely follows the analysis of Herrmann and Hölscher, but in one all-important respect he breaks away. While Hölscher denied the authorship of the greater part of the Book of Ezekiel, he still accepted the Exile framework. Herntrich repudiates this framework. On the same lines as Torrey and Smith, he shews how passage after passage presupposes the delivery of these prophetic speeches in person to the inhabitants of Judah and Jerusalem. The exiles are not 'the house of rebellion'; they are, according to Jeremiah (chapter xxiv), 'the good figs' as contrasted with the men of Judah and Jerusalem, who were 'the bad figs'. They were, in the main, true to Jehovah (Ezek. xi. 14–21). There are no references to the circumstances of these exiles in a strange land. The theme of the prophecies is uniformly (with the exception of three which are expressly addressed to the exiles) the sins of the people of Jerusalem and the inevitable 'end' which must ensue. Here in Jerusalem 'the rebellious house' is to be found. Here the prophet must have performed his symbolic acts and delivered his impassioned denunciations and appeals. What then are we to say as to the Babylonian framework? This is the work of an Editor of the Exile period. The vision of chapter i, the framing of the leading through the Temple in the shape of a transportation by the Spirit through the air to and from Jerusalem, the intrusion of chapters ix and x, all come from his hand. The original beginning of chapter i was manipulated so as to link it on to the vision. The Editor moreover transformed the account of the fugitive from Jerusalem (xxxiii. 21–23). Ezekiel lived either in the inner part of Jerusalem or more probably in the immediate neighbourhood and (in accordance with xxiv. 25–26) 'in the day' when the city fell, 'in that day' the fugitive came to bring the tidings (verse 27 is a gloss). But the Editor makes the fugitive come six months later to Babylon, the first to bring the tidings! When we enter chapters xl–xlviii, we find ourselves in another world, where the Temple worship is the absorbing topic. There are many contacts with the law of Holiness as a whole. The angel who conducts the Prophet is typical of the post-exilic literature. 'The prince' is quite a different person from the ideal 'David' of xxxiv. 23f., xxxvii. 24. He is an actual historical figure.

To go back to the original call of the genuine Ezekiel, this is to be found in iii. 22–23a, ii. 8ff. to iii. 9. The prophet is told to go into the plain (R.V.m. 'the valley' as xxxvii. 1, 2, Deut. xxxiv. 3, etc.). He sees a hand, holding out a roll, and he is bidden to eat it and is commissioned to speak its message to the house of Israel. Chapter iv (omit verse 6), v. 1–4, vi. 1–7, vii (text hopelessly corrupt), viii. 1, etc., 5–18, xi. 1–7, 11a, 13, belong to this original Text, xii–xxiv are in the main Ezekiel's, but with many corruptions and frequent later additions. Chapters xxv–xxxii (prophecies against foreign nations) are not his. Chapters xxxiiif., xxxvif. and ? xxxviiif. may be Ezekielian for the most part, spoken in exile. Chapters xl–xlviii are by the first Editor and by later hands.

Torrey, Smith and Herntrich have raised many important points, on which we must now endeavour to come to a decision.

CHAPTER V

CRITICISM OF DR JAMES SMITH'S THEORY

(i) On p. 27 we saw that Dr James Smith based his theory
that the original Ezekiel was a prophet of North Israel in
part upon the expression 'the house of Israel', as used in the
Book of Ezekiel. 'This phrase', he says, 'appears to refer to
the Northern Kingdom and to have no reference to Judah',*
and he quotes as 'an extraordinary statement' Herrmann's
declaration † that in iv. 1–3 'house of Israel' 'as always elsewhere in Ezekiel, designates the people of Judah' (iv. 4–6 being
an interpolation of later date). Dr Smith refers to five or six
passages in justification of his interpretation. But the phrase
occurs in Ezekiel eighty-three times. If these passages are
examined one by one and the indications, so far as they exist,
as to the persons meant by the phrase in each case are weighed,
it becomes evident that the words 'an extraordinary statement' used by Dr Smith of Herrmann's declaration (quoted
above) may with much more justification be applied to his
own.‡ The context shews that in the large majority of cases
the prophecies were used of the men of Judah and Jerusalem.
See iv. 3, v. 4, viii. 6, 10 ff., xi. 5, xii. 6, 27, xiii. 5, xvii. 2, xviii.
6–31, xx. 27–44, xxii. 18, xxiv. 21, xxix. 6, 16, 21, xxxiii. 7–20,
xxxv. 15. There can be little doubt that iv. 4–5 and ix. 9 also
refer to Judah, the specific references to Judah in iv. 6 and
ix. 9 being added by a later hand. Certain uses of the phrase

* Dr Smith, p. 56.   † Commentary, p. 31.
    ‡ See Excursus I, in which every passage in the Old Testament
in which 'the house of Israel' is used is set forth and discussed. The
uses in Ezekiel are to be found on pp. 93–101.

in passages primarily addressed to men of Jerusalem and Judah may at the same time well include men of the North, see vi. 11, xiv. 4, 11. In xx. 13 reference is made to 'the house of Israel' rebelling in the wilderness, where clearly the use answers to that which obtains in the P passages in the Pentateuch. In the later exilic and post-exilic chapters, the restored people are thought of as including men of the North and the South alike and as returning to possess the whole land of promise. See xxviii. 4f., xxxiv. 30, xxxvi. 10–37, xxxvii. 11, 16, xxxix. 12–29 and the passages in xl–xlviii. 'The house of Israel' (iii. 1–7) must be judged to have the same references as in the large majority of the passages. In xi. 15 the phrase is applied to the exiles and occurs in a late passage, which is certainly not Ezekiel's. There is in fact no genuine passage in which this phrase is certainly addressed to, or is a designation of, the Northern Kingdom alone. The use in xxxvii. 16 is in what is probably an insertion by a later hand and even there the MT reading is doubtful.

We must briefly consider other passages which Dr Smith regards as proofs that the Book of Ezekiel consists of prophecies addressed to the Northern Kingdom and not to Judah.

(ii) (p. 56) He understands viii. 6–16 as describing abominations committed by elders of the Northern Kingdom in the Temple at Jerusalem, and viii. 17 as an appeal to the elders of Judah (see verse 1) to repudiate the doings of the Northerners. But it is surely obvious that it is the prophet and not the house of Judah who is called upon to pass judgment and that the transgressors, called 'the house of Israel' in viii. 6–12 but in viii. 17 'the house of Judah', are the men of Jerusalem themselves. The author of chapters ix and x certainly thought so. The Northern Kingdom came to an end in 722 B.C. The prophet, according to practically universal opinion, is speaking about 590 B.C. The urgent matter was the imminent danger of the Southern Kingdom and its capital. Is it conceivable that the prophet should spend his energies upon the doings of a (supposed) body of elders of the remnant in the North and ignore the sins of Jerusalem? Even if we could accept the theory of Dr Smith that the prophet was really prophesying in the reign of Manasseh, is it conceivable that the Northerners (apparently) monopolized the Temple chambers with their portrayals and that Jehovah threatened to leave Jerusalem to destruction because of what these outsiders did? Dr Smith regards 'the house of Israel' in verses 6–12 as meaning Northern Israel only; would he in like manner confine 'the God of Israel' (viii. 4) to the North only (see ix. 3, x. 19f., xi. 22, xliii. 2, xliv. 2)?

(iii) (pp. 56–7) 'The residue (remnant) of Israel' in ix. 8 is regarded as 'signifying the pure Israelites of the Northern Kingdom' and states as a 'fact' that the number of Southerners deported from Jerusalem in 597 B.C. was small. For this last point Smith quotes Prof. Welch in *The People and the Book* (pp. 145–6). Welch depends here upon Jer. lii. 28, a remarkable passage which entirely contradicts 2 Kings xxiv. 15–16. It may be the more reliable, but it can hardly be assumed to be infallibly correct. But that is a minor point. The astonishing thing is that Smith should ignore 'the fact' that the phrase 'the remnant of Israel' occurs at the end of a vivid description of the slaughter of the people of Jerusalem, which so affected the prophet that he fell on his face and cried: 'Ah Lord Jehovah, wilt thou destroy all the residue of Israel in thy pouring out of thy fury upon Jerusalem?' Could anything be more perverse?

(iv) (p. 57) 'the distinction between Israel and Judah is evident.' Yes, as it stands. But see Excursus I, pp. 94–5.

(v) (p. 57) 'In xxi. 25 (K.H.B.) the reference is to Judah.' If this refers to xxi. 25 in MT (=verse 20 in LXX and E.V.)

the meaning of this statement is inexplicable. If it refers to xxi. 25 in LXX and E.V., it is quite true that the name 'prince of Israel' is given to the king of Judah, but the conclusion to be drawn from this is not that the Text should be arbitrarily emended, but that it should be recognized that Israel in Ezekiel's time was the regular designation for the remnant of God's people, who were still in the land.

(vi) (p. 57) 'In xxv. 3 a distinction is drawn between "the land of Israel" and "the house of Judah".' Is that so? 'The land of Israel' comes between 'my sanctuary' and 'the house of Judah'; is it not more natural to recognize that 'the land of Israel' means the *land* given to Israel of old, which still retained the old name although it had for long shrunk to the dimensions of the Southern Kingdom, while 'the house of Judah' means the *people* who occupied it.

(vii) (p. 57) 'In xxvii. 17 the distinction between the two Kingdoms is clear.' Surely not. Either, as in xxv. 3, 'Judah' means the people, 'the land of Israel' means the land Judah occupied, not a different land, or we may follow the LXX, which reads 'οἱ υἱοί of Israel', in which case Judah may be the land occupied by 'the children of Israel'.

(viii) (p. 57) 'In xxxvii. 16 the distinction is as clear as noonday.' See the note on this verse in Excursus I, p. 99 f.

(ix) (p. 57) 'There are other indications throughout the Book, which suggest that Ezekiel was a prophet of the North.' These indications are as unsubstantial as those which have gone before. These cannot be dealt with in detail here, but we may note the following: The simile of the vine in chapter xv is quoted as 'used by North Country prophets' (Hosea and Isaiah); it is *not* mentioned that the vine is used here as simile for 'the inhabitants of Jerusalem' (verse 6). 'The house of Jacob' (xx. 5, etc.) is regarded as standing for Northern

Israelites, because 'Jacob is the ancestor of Northern Israel'. Was he not, according to tradition, the ancestor of all Israel? Were only the Northern tribes brought out of Egypt (xx. 6 ff.)? Did they only receive Jehovah's statutes and rebel against him in the wilderness (xx. 11, 13)? xx. 34 is quoted as appropriate only to the exiles of the North, but verses 33–44 are an exilic prophecy of salvation at a time when Judah also is in captivity.

(x) Dr Smith puts forward certain dialectical peculiarities which he thinks indicate that Ezekiel is a prophet of the North: e.g. xxxvi. 13 אַתְּ. This occurs in Judges xvii. 2 (hill country of Ephraim), 1 Kings xiv. 2 (Jeroboam to his wife), 2 Kings iv. 16, 23, viii. 1 (the Shunemite) and Jer. iv. 30 (addressed to Jerusalem). In Ezek. xvi. 13 and nine times in that chapter the second person singular ending in תִּי instead of the תְּ of the Qri is found. This form is especially common in Jeremiah (ii. 33, iii. 4, 5, xxxi. 21, xlvi. 4). In both these cases the same argument would shew that Jeremiah also was 'a prophet of the North'!

It can be shewn on the other hand that the use of שׁ (=אֲשֶׁר), given by Dr Driver as an illustration of the way in which 'the language of North Israel differed slightly from Judaic Hebrew' (approximating in this particular to the dialect of Phoenicia), is never used by Ezekiel.

(xi) One more argument must be considered (pp. 66–9). 'The new Temple is not to be erected in Jerusalem. Ezekiel's sanctuary is to be erected "in the mountain of the height of Israel" (xx. 40). Had he contemplated Jerusalem as the site of the Temple of the future he would have said so. The author of Ezekiel xl–xlviii recognized that Ezekiel did not mean his Temple to be built on the Jerusalem site.' Mr Gaster is quoted as supporting the view that Ezekiel rejects Jerusalem as the site of the future Temple and selects a more central position

(*The Samaritans*, p. 15).* Can this argument be accepted as sound?

(*a*) Chapters xl–xlviii are an ideal picture of the future. The future Temple is seen as set upon 'a very high mountain' (xl. 2). One is reminded of Isaiah's picture (ii. 2) of 'the mountain of the house of Jehovah' as 'established upon the top of the mountains'. It is an ideal site, even as the partition of the land in chapter xlviii is an ideal partition, not corresponding in either case to any mundane position or measurements. Ezekiel, xvii. 22f., tells that when Jehoiachin and Zedekiah had been carried away into exile, Jehovah himself would plant a shoot of the cedar upon 'an high mountain and eminent', 'in the mountain of the height of Israel'. xix. 9 shews that 'the mountains of Israel' may be used in connection with a Judaean king (Jehoiachin). In xx. 40 we read: 'in mine holy mountain, in the mountain of the height of Israel, saith Lord Jehovah, there shall all the house of Israel, all of them, serve me...and there will I require your offerings... with all your holy things'. If 'my holy mountain' means the same as it does in Isaiah (xi. 9 = lxv. 25, lvi. 7, lvii. 13, lxv. 11, lxvi. 20; cf. xxvii. 13 and Jer. xxxi. 23) it must mean 'my holy mountain Jerusalem'. Dr Smith says that 'the mountain of the height of Israel' to 'an unbiassed mind can have but one interpretation—the mountain land of Ebal and Gerizim'. It seems much more probable that this expression, in the three passages in which it occurs (xvii. 22ff., xx. 40, xxxiv. 14), is a general term, referring to the central line of hills, which forms the backbone of Palestine, and which extended to the south of Hebron.

(*b*) In the same way the partition of the land into 'the holy portion' with the city and the prince's portions adjoining

* See also article in *C.Q.R.* Jan. 1935, 'The Key of the Old Testament', by Cameron Mackay.

(xlv. 1–8, xlviii. 8–22), and into the twelve tribal areas on the west side of the Jordan, is a symmetrical scheme, having little, if any, thought of its practical working out. The northern and southern borders of the land are given, but (xlviii. 1–7 and 23–29) the size of the several portions is left quite indefinite. It is a purely arbitrary supposition that the portions were 'equal' or were 'strips of equal width'. The tribes were never all of equal size and such tribes as Simeon and Reuben had in reality long ceased to have a separate existence. The author of these last nine chapters of Ezekiel, like the author of Revelation (vii. 5–8), thinks of Israel in its ideal completeness as 'the twelve-tribed nation' (Acts xxvi. 7). It is quite vain to seek to discover the geographical situation of the future Temple, as imagined by the Prophet, from arithmetical calculations based on this idealized picture.

We may sum up this discussion by saying that, so far from the evidence adduced 'in favour of the theory that Ezekiel was a North Israelite and that the appeal of his book was directed to the North Israelite community' being 'unanswerable' (p. 71), it would seem on critical examination to be fatally weak and inconclusive.

Chapter VI

CRITICISM OF DR TORREY'S THEORY

The main *plank* in the platform of Dr Torrey's argument (see pp. 23–27) is his interpretation of chapter i. 1–4 and especially of the mysterious date 'the thirtieth year'. This, therefore, I propose to discuss in this chapter, but to deal with it in the course of a more general discussion on the datings to be found in the whole Book of Ezekiel.

1. A study of the use of the numerals in Ezekiel seems to point to the conclusion that the datings were not all by the same hand or in the same generation.

(i) In viii. 1, xx. 1, xxiv. 1 and xxix. 1 the usage is בַּשָּׁנָה followed by ordinal numbers.

(ii) But in i. 1, xxvi. 1, xxix. 17, xxx. 20, xxxi. 1, xxxii. 1, 17, xxxiii. 21, xl. 1 the numeral comes first and שָׁנָה follows.

(iii) Whereas בְּאַחַת עֶשְׂרֵה is the Hebrew for 'eleventh' in xxx. 20 and xxxi. 1, the form בְּעַשְׁתֵּי עֶשְׂרֵה is used in xxvi. 1. This form seems to be a loan word from the Babylonian and was gradually substituted for the earlier form. It occurs in MT only in Jer. i. 3 (in Editorial preface), xxxix. 2 = lii. 5 = 2 Kings xxv. 2 (which is probably the original and by the younger Editor D²; note the late usage as to months), Zech. i. 7, six times in P (Exod. and Num.), five times in 1 Chronicles and twice in Ezekiel (xxvi. 1, xl. 49).

2. The usage in some parts of Ezekiel departs from the usual rules for numerals in several particulars:

(i) Whereas numbers 2–10 regularly take the noun numbered in the plural, in xlv. 1 we find רֹחַב עֲשָׂרָה אֶלֶף. (Possibly this may be due to its being immediately preceded by וְעֶשְׂרִים אֶלֶף

אֹרֶךְ חֲמִשָּׁה. Also the LXX here has 'twenty'.) The same usage is found in the Kthiv of 2 Kings viii. 17 שָׁנָה and xxv. 17 אַמָּה, both passages being Editorial (D¹ and D²).

(ii) Numerals 11–19 are usually followed by the plural, but words frequently used with numerals, such as אִישׁ, are used commonly in the singular. The tens (20 to 90), when they precede, take the singular of the same class of nouns, such as אֶלֶף, and so in Ezekiel and as a rule in P שֶׁקֶל (Ezek. iv. 10), but otherwise they take the plural. In Ezek. xlv. 12, however, שְׁקָלִים follows both עֶשְׂרִים and חֲמִשָּׁה וְעֶשְׂרִים, though in the same verse שֶׁקֶל follows עֲשָׂרָה וַחֲמִשָּׁה.

(iii) After מֵאָה etc., אַמָּה etc. regularly occur in the singular, but in xl. 27 we find מֵאָה אַמּוֹת.

(iv) The thousands regularly precede the hundreds, etc.; but xlviii. 16, חֲמֵשׁ מֵאוֹת וְאַרְבַּעַת אֲלָפִים, occurs four times and xlviii. 30, 32 ff. the same.

(v) The hundreds almost always precede the smaller numbers, and so Ezek. iv. 5–9 שְׁלֹשׁ־מֵאוֹת וְתִשְׁעִים יוֹם, but in xlviii. 17 we find חֲמִשִּׁים וּמָאתַיִם four times; cf. 1 Kings ix. 23, '50 and 500', x. 29, '50 and 100'. 1 Kings ix. 23 occurs in a passage, which is not found at this point in LXX (B), but which occurs in partial form between x. 22 and x. 23; x. 29 according to this order follows closely upon it and appears to be due to the same writer; contrast in the same context ix. 14, 28, x. 10, 14, where the regular order obtains. In vi. 1 the object is repeated, '80 year and 400 year'. In P this becomes the rule, as Gen. v. 3, 6ff., 10f., 13f., etc. (but in verse 5 the reverse order prevails, '900 year and 30 year', which may be an insertion).

(vi) In the case of tens and units, the earlier books put the tens before the units, but in Ezek. xl. 2, 25, 30, 33 we find the reverse order '5 and 20 cubits', in xlv four times and xlviii eleven times ('5 and 20 thousand') and once (xlv. 12) '5 and 20 shekels', but in the same verse we have also '10 and

5 shekels' (cf. Jer. xxv. 3 'three and twenty', xxxii. 9 '7 shekels and 10' and lii. 30 'three and twentieth year'). The earlier usage is, however, also found in Ezek. xi. 1, xxix. 17, xl. 1, 13, 29 (and so Jer. lii. 1, 28 ff.).

(vii) 'By the cubit' (בָּאַמָּה), xl. 5, 21, xlvii. 3, is a phrase found also in 1 Kings vi. 6, 17, 25, vii. 23 f., 27, 31, 38, Exod. xxvi. 2, xxxvi. 9, 15, xxxviii. 9, 14 f., Num. xxxv. 5 (P seven times), Zech. v. 2, 1 Chron. xi. 23, 2 Chron. iv. 2 f.

It is significant that the above exceptional uses in Ezekiel almost all fall in chapters xl–xlviii, but it must also be remembered that, except in regard to dates, numerals only rarely occur in chapters i–xxxix. Moreover, while the variations may indicate different hands or times of writing, they may also indicate that the time of writing was transitional and that the writer indifferently used the older and the newer methods.

3. If we study the datings separately from other enumerations, we see that they fall into two classes:

(i) In three passages the starting-point is stated: i. 2 In the fifth year of Jehoiachin's captivity. xxxiii. 21 In the twelfth year of our captivity. xl. 1 In the twenty and fifth year of our captivity.

(ii) In the other ten passages no starting-point is named. One of these dates, however, can be identified, for in chapter xxiv. 1 the Prophet is bidden to write down the day as being the day on which the king of Babylon invested Jerusalem (סָמַךְ used intransitively as in Psalm lxxxviii. 8 (7)). 2 Kings xxv. 1 tells us that this event occurred in the ninth year of king Zedekiah. The dating in Ezekiel and in 2 Kings exactly correspond, and it is clear that Ezekiel's ninth year is the ninth year of Zedekiah. Here we seem to have the clue to the other datings of the second group. They all take the accession of Zedekiah as their starting-point, and are earlier than the three datings which start from the captivity of Jehoiachin and which reflect an exilic standpoint. It may be argued that the two sets of datings may really all be reckoned from the same starting-point, but it is very improbable that the exiles would reckon their years of exile from the enthronement of the Zedekiah who supplanted their own exiled king. If, as is argued in Chapter IV, p. 24f., the genuine prophecies of the Book, relating prophecies prior to the destruction of Jerusalem, were delivered by the prophet in person to the inhabitants of that city, then it is clear that the second class of datings would take as their starting-point the enthronement of Zedekiah and not the commencement of the Exile. xxiv. 1–14 corresponds to the situation in Jerusalem at the time. 'The selfsame day' is a characteristic phrase in P (Gen. vii. 13 and ten times), also found in Deut. xxxii. 48, Josh. v. 11 and x. 27 (in all three passages R^P has been at work) and three times in Ezek. ii. 3, xxiv. 2, xl. 1. In all probability 'this selfsame day the king of Babylon invested the Jerusalem this selfsame day' (xxiv. 2) is an explanatory insertion by an Editorial hand, though possibly it may have been added by Ezekiel himself at a later date. The words explain the command to note down this particular day.

4. The date given in the present text of i. 1 has been the despair of commentators. Hölscher regards it as secondary and that in verse 2 as primary, because the former stands alone; it is abandoned in the next dated passage and never taken up again. This thirtieth year in Hölscher's opinion cannot be fitted in with the fifth year of Jehoiachin's captivity. It cannot be the age of the prophet nor the thirtieth year from the starting of the Josianic Reform. He agrees with Duhm that a Midrashic Editor has calculated it by deducting Ezekiel's 'forty years' (iv. 6) from Jeremiah's 'seventy years' (Jer. xxv. 11–12, xxix. 10). Herrmann follows Kraetzschmar, Jahn, Budde, etc. in regarding i. 1 as original and i. 2 as a gloss. The

chronology of i. 1 at a later date was not understood and i. 2 was added as explanation. i. 1 a is the beginning of the original call narrative, i. 1 b introduces the vision of i. 4–28, which was added to the chapter at a later date by an Editor. It is due to this editing that the Text is found in its present disordered state. 'The heavens were opened' has no parallel either in Ezekiel or in any part of the Old Testament. (The phrase occurs in later writings, 3 Maccabees vi. 18, Mark i. 10, Apocalypse of St John, etc.) Both this phrase and 'the visions of God' (again viii. 3, xl. 2) are of questionable genuineness. Herrmann frankly abandons any hope of a certain solution of the era involved.

Torrey (see p. 23) confidently affirms that the thirtieth year is the thirtieth year of king Manasseh. This is devoid of solid foundation. But we must give consideration here to his solution of the dislocation which has taken place in i. 1–4. The original Text, he says, was i. 1 a and c, 4 and possibly 'the hand of Jehovah was upon me'. The following are Editorial additions: 'and I was in the midst of the Exiles at the river Chebar', 'in the fifth to the month, i.e. the fifth year of the exile of king Jehoiachin, the word of Jehovah came to Ezekiel, son of Buzi the priest in the land of the Chaldeans at the river Chebar'.

The Editor thus transferred to Babylonia during the years of Jehoiachin's captivity the prophecies which were originally uttered in the days of king Manasseh. But could an Editor, as able as (according to Torrey) this man was, have been content to produce such a chaos as we have in the present Text? Can we imagine him breaking into the narrative of the prophet which was in the first person by a passage in the third person (verses 2 and 3)? Could he have deliberately left the dating 'in the thirtieth year' hanging in the air without any definition of the era? Could the same man, who executed the alteration of place by inserting in verse 1 'as I was...Chebar' have thought it necessary to insert in verse 3, so close to the first, a second statement to the same effect in the third person?

Budde, who asks the above questions, provides a much more reasonable solution of the problem.* The passage in verse 3 shews every sign of having been intruded into its present position by some wooden-headed copyist without any regard to sense or context. But, if so, how did the latter come by it? Note the remarkable fact that the Book of Ezekiel, as it stands, is unique among the Hebrew prophetical writings in that it has no superscription. Hebrew Editors have placed at the head of each collection of a prophet's speeches a statement in the third person as to the writer and his time. Four of these superscriptions begin: 'The word of Jehovah, which came unto....' Five begin: 'The word of Jehovah came unto...,' and in three of these cases the date (year, month and (once) day) is put in the forefront. 'The burden of the word of Jehovah to Israel' occurs four times and 'The vision (or 'the words') which...saw' five times. Now in Ezek. i. 3 we find a similar statement: 'The word of Jehovah came unto Ezekiel,' etc. Is not this part of a superscription which originally stood at the head of the collection?

We notice further that in Jeremiah the superscription in the third person is immediately followed by the prophet's own narrative of his call in the first person. The same phenomenon probably appeared also in Isaiah, if (with Prof. Budde) we take it that the narrative of the prophet's call in the first person, now found in chapter vi, originally stood immediately after the Editorial superscription. Very possibly in like manner Hosea iii once stood immediately after the superscription in i. 1. By analogy we should expect that the Book of Ezekiel would also be furnished with an Editorial superscription (now found

* *Expository Times*, Oct. 1900, Aug. and Oct. 1901 and *J.B.L.* vol. L, part ii, 1931.

in verse 3) and that it might be followed by a narrative of Ezekiel's call in the first person (i. 1, 4, etc.).

But if this be accepted, there still remain three points which require elucidation:

(*a*) Verse 2 begins: 'In the fifth day of the month which was the fifth year....' To what does the relative refer back? Grammatically, as it stands, it can only refer back to the preceding 'day' or 'month', but that makes nonsense. It must have referred back to a 'year' previously mentioned. What could that year be but the year in i. 1? If so, this note 'which is the fifth year' must now stand in the wrong place. Must it not have originally been a note in the margin, and must not the preceding words, 'in the fifth day of the month', have been repeated from verse 1 and have been placed before this marginal note to shew what it referred to? We to-day would put an asterisk and a footnote. Then later on it would seem that the compound marginal note was inserted as a whole into its present position by an unintelligent copyist.

(*b*) As soon as this marginal note became part of the Text, it would be seen that it manifestly required that a statement should follow, declaring what happened 'in the fifth day...'. For this purpose it would seem that the original superscription was transferred to its present position, for thus the requirement would be fully met.

(*c*) There still remains the crux of the whole passage: 'the thirtieth year'—of what? Torrey says that it originally ran: 'in the thirtieth year of king Manasseh' and that the later Editor omitted the last words. We cannot, however, suppose that this Editor would have left the passage as it now stands. If he inserted 'which was in the fifth year...', the preceding words must have expressed some definite date, which was thus further identified with the fifth year of the better-known era of the Captivity. But no other era has been found, whose thirtieth year synchronized with this 'fifth year'. There are, however, two possible solutions still to be considered. Seventeen hundred years ago Origen propounded the theory that the thirtieth year might be that of the prophet's own life. This is the solution which Prof. Budde adopts. In 1900 he suggested that the gap was originally filled by לְחַיַּ ('of my life') on the lines of Gen. vii. 11. In 1931 he put forward a still simpler solution, viz. to read שְׁנַי ('my years') instead of שָׁנָה ('year'), which gives the sense 'the thirtieth of my years'.* Two objections have been raised to this: (α) in Hebrew usage a man's age is generally expressed by saying that he was 'son of... years', and (β) that the addition of month and day suggests a regnal year rather than an individual's life year. These difficulties are real, but not insuperable (see Budde's answers in the *Expository Times*, 1901), and the solution as a whole has the advantage that it places the whole material of i. 1–4 in an intelligible order, analogous to the introductory verses of other prophetical Books, and explains in a reasonable manner all the difficulties which confront us in the existing Text.

The latest solution is propounded by Herntrich (*Ezechiel-probleme*, p. 63). He suggests that the original reading was שְׁלִישִׁי (third),† which was corrupted into שְׁלִישִׁים (thirty), and he supports this by an ingenious argument to shew that the third year of the Zedekiah era would be equivalent, in the Palestinian calendar, to the fifth year of the Captivity, calculated according to the Babylonian method of reckoning from the spring instead of from the autumn. One difficulty of this solution is that 'the third year' would normally in Hebrew be 'in the year the third' as in viii. 1, xx. 1, xxiv. 1, xxix. 1

---

* Cf. Ps. xxxi. 11 (E.V. 10) 'my years with sighing', and Isa. xxxviii. 10 'the residue of my years', etc.

† But would this be possible Hebrew?

and not in the order of the present text of i. 1 'in the thirty year' as in xxx. 20, xxxii. 1, etc.

On the whole we seem shut up to the conclusion that no solution is free from difficulty and that it is questionable whether we can ever now arrive at certainty in this matter.

CHAPTER VII

FURTHER CRITICISM OF TORREY'S THEORY

(i) Who were the sinners denounced by Ezekiel? In the next chapter we shall see that the prophecies bear many marks, which seem to shew that they were spoken to the generation of Zedekiah. But Torrey (see pp. 23, 26f.) will have it that they are fictitious prophecies, which in their original form professed to be addressed to the Judaeans of the reign of Manasseh.

If we ask how was an author living and writing in 230 B.C. able to find the material out of which to weave the whole series of prophecies and to utter these tremendous denunciations, Torrey replies that he found it in 2 Kings xxi. 2–16, which enumerates the sins of Manasseh and tells how Jehovah's servants the prophets poured out threatenings against that evil generation. When, however, we compare the Book of Ezekiel with these few verses in 2 Kings, we find it difficult, if not impossible, to conceive how so massive and impressive a book could have been built up upon so slight a foundation, or that the author would have adopted so roundabout a method of delivering his message to his own contemporaries. And there is this serious flaw in the theory, viz. that, whereas 2 Kings xxi–xxiv lays such particular and repeated stress upon the guilt of king Manasseh, not one single line in Ezekiel points to such a figure. The 'bloody city' (xxii. 2, xxiv. 6–9, etc.), the house of Israel, its princes and rulers, the inhabitants of Jerusalem, all these are denounced unsparingly for their idolatries and sins, but never once is Manasseh hinted at or the word 'king' used in that connection. If the weak but well-

meaning Zedekiah was king when these prophecies were delivered, this is intelligible; on Torrey's supposition it seems
inexplicable. Moreover, the picture of idolatrous worship in
secret chambers of imagery does not suggest the barefaced
pollution of the Temple by Manasseh, and here again there
is no picture of the guilty king, but of groups of men and
women, '70 elders', of whom two are mentioned by name.*
Furthermore, it is a question whether 2 Kings (especially
xxiii. 26f. and xxiv. 3f.) can be relied upon, as Torrey would
suggest. A study of these chapters gives the impression that
the writer is seeking to whitewash his own generation. *They*
were not, he says in effect, the guilty ones. The last generation
was doomed from the first. Even the good work done by
Josiah had not been sufficient to wipe out Manasseh's guilt.
He and he alone was responsible. 'The fathers had eaten sour
grapes and the children's teeth were set on edge.' The writer
of these last chapters of 2 Kings in fact expresses the very view
which Ezekiel combats in chapters xviii and xxxiii. Ezekiel's
whole message in these chapters seems to be intended to bring
home to that last generation that it was their own persistency
in wrongdoing, and not the sins of a past generation, which
was bringing down upon them the wrath of the God of righteousness. It is hardly consistent for Torrey to rely so implicitly
upon 2 Kings, when it suits his theory, and then to turn round
at another time and accuse the writer of 'unhappy exaggera-
tion', when in the same context he makes statements of the

* As a matter of fact, Millar Burrows in his essay on *The Literary
Relations of Ezekiel* does not find one single reference to 2 Kings xxi
on which the Book of Ezekiel is said to be based. The oracles on the
false prophets in xii. 24, xiii. 6ff., xxii. 28 are said to be based on
2 Kings xxi. 6, but not one of the varieties of divination in that verse
are once mentioned in Ezekiel and characteristic phrases in 2 Kings
xxi. 8 and 13, describing the prophetic messages of the prophets of
Manasseh's days, are not used by Ezekiel.

large numbers who went into captivity with Jehoiachin and with Zedekiah (2 Kings xxiv. 14–16 and xxv. 11–12). The evidence forthcoming both from Jeremiah (e.g. vii. 31) and Ezekiel (e.g. xx. 31 '...unto this day') that Moloch worship and other idolatries were rampant in their own day, in spite of the elaborate attempts made by Torrey (*Pseudo-Ezekiel*, pp. 48–57), is too strong to be overthrown.

Dr Torrey's remaining arguments can only be briefly dealt with.

(ii) It is true that Jeremiah seems to be ignored by Ezekiel, but what Hebrew prophet is there who does mention by name a contemporary or nearly contemporary prophet? Isaiah does not mention Micah, or Hosea Amos, nor Jeremiah Hosea; and yet e.g. Jeremiah seems clearly to borrow from Hosea. See Jer. iv. 3 and Hos. x. 12; Jer. iii. 22 and Hosea xiv. 5 (E.V. 4).

(iii) As for the mention of Persians and the supposed knowledge of Alexander the Great, Torrey, whose Editor inserted so many references to Babylonia, cannot complain, if we point out with Hölscher that the reference in chapter xxvii to Persians in the army of Tyre occurs in that prose section which is clearly a later insertion and that the similar reference in chapter xxxviii may equally be the work of a late hand. Apart from that, Shalom Spiegel* points out that on an obelisk of Shalmanezer (? 835 B.C.) mention is made of the Madai (Medes) and the country Parsna. Made an Assyrian province in 744 B.C., Parsna is frequently mentioned in later records. The obscure passage in viii. 17 ('branch to nose') is not as Torrey says (p. 84) a 'plain allusion to Persian ritual', nor is it possible to explain why the innocent custom, supposed to be referred to, should be branded as the basest of all abominations.† As

* Article in the *Harvard Theological Review*, Oct. 1931.

† Spiegel in his article (p. 300) gives the true account of the Persian rite.

to Gog himself, we have only to read Gressmann and Herrmann
on chapters xxxviii–xxxix to see that this Apocalyptic figure
is probably modelled upon a Babylonian mythical hero and
to realize the precariousness of an identification with any
actual king of history.

(iv) The argument from the undoubted Aramaic colouring
of the Book of Ezekiel is also precarious. On the one hand we
have books of the second century B.C. which are written in
much purer Hebrew, and on the other hand it is quite credible
that residence in Babylonia in his later years gave the Aramaic
colouring. It is noteworthy that while Torrey claims that these
Aramaicisms pervade the whole Book, this is not the case. They
congregate closely in certain chapters such as the thirteenth
and these are just the passages which Hölscher for example
assigns to his secondary hand. Here again Spiegel shews how
widely Aramaic had currency in Babylonia. For example,
weights and measures about 700 B.C. drop the Assyrian termi-
nology and retain only the Aramaic. It was only due to the
stubbornness of religious teachers among the Hebrews that
Hebrew survived at all among the captives. The Aramaic
element in the Book in fact seems to prove the Babylonian
editing of the work. But even in Palestine the Hebrew of
Ezekiel's earlier and later contemporaries shews similar ten-
dencies.* Babylonian loan words seem only to be explicable
as derived from Babylonian environment.†

(v) The argument from literary dependence cannot be
relied upon. The question whether Ezekiel or Leviticus and
Second Isaiah and Job and Daniel came first cannot be proved

---

* See Jer. xii. 5, xxii. 15, xxv. 34 and so II Isaiah.

† E.g. Ezek. xii. 14 + 6 times אֲנַפִּים; xl. 22 אֵלַמּוֹ Kthiv + 12
times = 'porch'; xvi. 33 וְדָנַיְה, xix. 9 סוּגַר and see Spiegel, p. 304f.;
also, p. 307, 'Nar Kabari' (= Khebar) found on contract tablets
and with a number of genuine Jewish names of customers.

by internal evidence alone. Torrey says that it is 'plain fact' that Ezekiel knew both our Book of 'Job' and the primitive Daniel, but Millar Burrows says there is no evidence that Ezekiel knew the poem of Job. He finds dependence on Ezekiel in the Hebrew part of Daniel, while its 'Aramaic portion may well be prior to Ezekiel'.

(vi) As regards the date of writing, the prophecies fit naturally into the period round about the end of the Kingdom and the beginning of the Exile, whereas there are other passages, which, if written (as Torrey would have us believe) about 230 B.C., are quite inexplicable. Torrey says that shortly before that date the Northern Kingdom of the Seleucids was crumbling. How then, says Spiegel (p. 318), could Ezekiel foretell that the Northern Kingdom would crush the powerful Egypt so as to leave it uninhabited and henceforth to be the basest of the Kingdoms? The silence as to Babylonia is natural in a prophecy spoken or edited on Babylonian soil, but very strange, if written under Egyptian rule, and if accompanied by denunciations of the dominant power in the Palestine of that day.

(vii) Finally, we must briefly deal with the value of that 'oldest Jewish tradition' to which Torrey appeals as shewing that it 'recognizes no Babylonian prophet Ezekiel', and that 'they knew that the Book was not written by the Ezekiel of the Babylonian Captivity'. The matter is fully dealt with from the point of view of Talmudic and Rabbinic learning by Shalom Spiegel in the article already quoted, in which he states that one defect in Torrey's argument is that 'it rests on nothing'.

The Jewish Doctors did not hide their real reasons for decision by 'good-humoured camouflage'. They were in deadly earnest. The Law was eternally valid. Not even the remote future could bring a new law. By sometimes desperate violence

4-2

to the language of the Text Rabbinic ingenuity found a way of reconciling what appeared to be contradictions. The hesitation to admit Ezekiel into the Canon was not due to any doubt as to the genuineness of the Book, but to the difficulty of reconciling some passages with the Levitical Law and to the danger to immature minds of the study of the lore of the mystic chariot, as described in chapter i. It was therefore laid down that 'the works of the chariot' were not to be discussed at all. The chapter was, however, preserved as being the prophet's answer to the question: Will God survive His Sanctuary? Ezekiel saw God carried away in His chariot to the heavenly abode. Spiegel's whole discussion is illuminating and should be read in its entirety. It must suffice here to ask what is the treatise on which Torrey bases so startling a statement.

The Baba Bathra * cannot be much, if at all, earlier than the sixth century A.D., i.e. some ten centuries after Ezra and Nehemiah. Its statements are absolutely uncritical. Samuel, for example, is said to have 'written his own book', although not his death, but the appearance of his spirit after death to Saul at Endor is recorded before the end of the first half of the book. Jeremiah is allowed to have written his own book, but 'Hezekiah and his company wrote Isaiah, Proverbs, the Song of Songs and the Preacher'. In Prov. xxv. 1 we read 'These also are proverbs of Solomon, which the men of Hezekiah... copied out'. To the writer of the Baba Bathra this mention of a company of scribes was a lucky find and he therefore ascribed to them not only Proverbs xxv–xxix but also i–xxiv and, further, other books which by this time were ascribed to Solomon. To these was added Isaiah, because he was contemporary with Hezekiah. This throws vivid light upon what

* A translation of the whole passage is given in Ryle's *Canon of the Old Testament*, Excursus B; see also *Enc. Bibl.*, "Canon of the O.T." §§ 18–21 and Budde's article in *J.B.L.* vol. L, part ii, 1931.

the writer meant by 'wrote'. The Holy Spirit was the real author of Scripture. He might use Isaiah as his original mouthpiece, but afterwards he could dictate the prophecies to any scribe whom he might choose. In this sense Isaiah was 'written' by the men of Hezekiah, and 'Ezekiel, etc.' were written by the men of the great synagogue. Who were these? The earliest reference to such a body is in the Pirqe Aboth (second or third century A.D.). The Rabbis felt it to be so essential to shew that the true tradition had been preserved that they seem to have filled up the huge gap between Ezra and Simon the Just by transforming the great assembly of Neh. viii. 10 into a great synagogue of eighty-five men. Still later they seized upon this great synagogue as a company who could do for Ezekiel and the Twelve what Hezekiah's men did for Isaiah. To attempt to gather reliable evidence as to the date of Ezekiel from this hopelessly uncritical document is in Prof. Budde's words to seek to 'gather grapes from thorns'. The final judgment on Dr Torrey's ingenious construction must be that it is built upon precarious foundations and fails to carry conviction.

CHAPTER VIII

THE SEPARATION OF THE EDITORIAL ADDITIONS FROM THE ORIGINAL EZEKIELIAN PROPHECIES

We have already seen how Herrmann and Hölscher propose to make the solution. I propose now to take two or three sections of the Book and to consider how far the clue propounded by Herntrich (see pp. 29f.) satisfies this problem.

We will first take chapters i–iii which relate the Vision and the Call. We have seen that Prof. Budde would explain i. 1–4 as consisting of an original narrative of the prophet's call (verses 1 and 4), a superscription and marginal notes, which were subsequently introduced into the Text in wrong places. But what is the relation of the original beginning to the rest of chapter i? Herntrich replies that the original beginning ran as follows: 'And it came to pass in the [third] year in the fourth [month] in the fifth day of the month and the word of Jehovah came to Ezekiel, the son of Buzi the priest and the hand of Jehovah was upon him.' This would form a suitable introduction to the whole Book, but not to the vision which immediately follows. What then is the explanation of the rest of the present verses 1–3? The answer is that i. 1 c 'the heavens were opened and I saw visions of God' is the superscription to the *Vision*. This was the work of a later writer, who worked in his own composition to form part of the narrative of the prophetic call. Verse 4 links on naturally to i. 1 b by its taking up of the phrase at the end of that half verse, 'and I saw visions of God', 'and I saw and behold'. At the same time the statement was added: 'and I was in the midst of the captivity by the river Chebar' and (verse 2) the explanation of the date. Other glosses were subsequently added (3 b 'in the land of the Chaldeans by the river Chebar' and 'there'). The pre-exilic prophet had no need to give an exact geographical description of the country in which the word of Jehovah came to him. Moreover, it is strange that the prophet should see this vision 'in the midst of the captivity' and iii. 15 says that it was only when the Spirit of Jehovah 'took him away' that he 'came to them of the captivity at Tel-abib that dwelt by the river Chebar'. Also the word 'there' is wanting in the LXX. Almost always in Ezekiel this word is textually uncertain and seems to be a gloss.

Herrmann and Hölscher both separate the description of the throne-chariot from the original narrative (the one separates verses 6–26, the other verses 5–27). It is better, with Herntrich, to separate verses 4–28b (down to 'the glory of Jehovah') as composing one whole, and i. 28c to ii. 2 'and, when I saw it, I fell upon my face and I heard a voice of one that spake...' as an Editorial addition to link on the vision to the subsequent call. The call is contained in ii–iii, but with the original call is combined other matter, partly perhaps Ezekiel's, partly by a later hand, the whole being put together with little regard to true order. Things stand together which have no connection, things which belong together are separated by foreign matter, sometimes two versions of the same theme seem to have been placed near one another. ii. 6–iii. 9 seem to contain the genuine account of the call. iii. 22–23a is the original introduction to it. The prophet is told to go into the valley-plain. There Jehovah will speak with him.* The words of viii. 4 'and behold, the glory of the God of Israel was there, according to the appearance that I saw in the plain' suggest that this 'appearance' or vision in the plain was given with

* Cf. 'the hand of Jehovah was upon him' (omit 'there') in i. 3c. The word 'valley-plain' is the one used in Gen. xi. 2, Deut. xxxiv. 3, Josh. xi. 8, 17, etc. It occurs again in viii. 4 and xxxvii. 1–2.

greater wealth of detail in the original account which followed on iii. 22–23a, but that this was superseded by the vision of the later writer in chapter i, which is referred back to by the addition 'as the glory which I saw by the river Chebar' in ii. 23b. The actual call then is given in ii. 6–iii. 9. iii. 10–15 is a later addition. The prophet in the original narrative is sent to 'the house of Israel' (iii. 1, 4f., 7), but now (according to iii. 11) he is said to be sent to the Captivity, the Spirit has to lift him up and carry him to the river Chebar, the Vision of chapter i recurs and stands in contrast to the vision of the hand and of the roll (ii. 9ff.) which is part of the genuine narrative of the Call. This original narrative is quite in the line of the great prophets. On the other hand i. 4–28 is a literary composition, and the passages in ii–iii not included in iii. 22f. and ii. 6–iii. 9 have been added later.

The next passage, which we select for discussion, is chapters viii–xi. They now form a unity, but recent critics agree that some part is later addition. Herrmann says: 'We have a literary unity before us, which has been burst through by a foreign body.' And this is the opinion also of Hölscher and Herntrich. But there is difference of opinion on the question as to what part is original and what is the 'foreign body'. All agree that xi. 14–21 is not part of this Temple section and Herrmann also rejects xi. 1–13 on the ground that ix. 8 tells of the carrying out of the judgment on the men of distinction, leaving no room for the activities of the twenty-five leaders of the people, as given in xi. 1ff. Further, Herrmann rejects chapter x as not part of the original vision, as at the best being so glossed as to be in an incurable condition. The identification of the 'living creatures' of chapter i with the 'cherubim' in chapter x may be intended to distinguish them from the colossal door-guarding beasts of Assyria and to assimilate them to the cherubim in the Temple. The pollution of the Temple in chapter viii on reflection seems to have convinced Ezekiel that Jehovah must leave his sanctuary (chapter ix), and in order to present this in an imposing manner he reintroduces the conception of the glory of Jehovah and of the throne-chariot and adds it to the original vision. xi. 22–25 also belongs to the conceptions of chapter x.

Hölscher agrees with Herrmann that 'the original stock' is contained in chapters viii–ix and he regards xi. 22–25 as its completion, but even these two chapters have been freely edited and worked over, especially the typographical notes. The original Ezekielian passages probably were viii. 1–3, 5–6, 7, 9, 17, ix. 1–7, 11, xi. 24–25.

Herntrich takes a different line. Chapter x, he says, cannot be struck out and chapter ix be retained. The two chapters are organically bound together. Moreover, chapters viii and xi. 1–13 are bound together by the passages viii. 7, 14, 16, xi. 1, which tell how Ezekiel is 'brought' from one part of the Temple to another. Chapters ix and x by their 'Phantasy Visions' break this connection. The original vision comes to a climax in xi. 13, which tells how Pelatiah, when he heard Ezekiel's prophecy, fell dead. This was not a vision, but a real event in Jerusalem. A Babylonian Editor subsequently placed a visionary framework round it. viii. 1–4 shews the hand of the same later Editor as do the Editorial additions in i. 1–3. The statement of place in Babylonia always appears in conjunction with fragments of the vision in i. 4–28. In viii. 1 'there' and probably 'as I sat in mine house and the elders of Judah sat before me' are added to the original opening words. 'Fell' (viii. 1) should probably be 'was' (so LXX and Vulg.) as in i. 3.*

---

* In verse 2 the word translated in E.V. 'colour' is lit. 'eye'. It is used in late Hebrew in the sense of appearance or gleam, as in i. 4, 7, 16, 22, 27, x. 9, Dan. x. 6, Lev. xiii. 5, 37, 55, Num. xi. 7, and the word for 'amber' has the Aramaic emphatic ending.

The opening words of viii. 3 a seem to be an imitation of
ii. 9 a and 'the spirit' is in harmony with iii. 12, 14. 'The
visions of God' links on to i. 1 c. The rest of viii. 3 and 4 is
a gloss. Verses 5–6 are the Divine Speech as given in the
original and verse 7 speaks of the bringing of the prophet by
natural means to the door of the court. Chapter ix breaks
into the original narrative and narrates the judgment on
Jerusalem in Babylonian myth-drapery. Chapter x falls into
line with chapter ix. Its description of the cherubim cannot
be fully harmonized with the description of the living creatures
in i. 4–28. It seems clearly to be Editorial. Chapter xi. 1–13
is in the main Ezekielian, but in xi. 1 'the spirit lifted me up
and brought me' has been substituted for 'he brought me',
in xi. 5 'and the spirit of Jehovah fell upon me' has been
added, and in xi. 8–10 and 11 b–12 we seem to have secondary
elements. xi. 14–21 is clearly later insertion and is doubtfully
from Ezekiel. xi. 22–25 are the handiwork of the later writer,
who transferred the whole vision to Babylonia.

Space forbids the consideration of further passages on the
same scale, but the following notes will serve to indicate how
the application of the same clue restores the earlier prophecies
to a natural situation, viz. as pre-exilic addresses to Jerusalem.

Chapter xii (see Torrey above, p. 24). The symbolic actions
could only have been effective if carried out in Jerusalem
before 586 B.C. 'I am your sign' (verse 11) and the second
person in verse 20 have been left unaltered by the Editor, and
they shew that originally the verbs in verse 19 were also in
the second person in harmony with the initial words 'say unto
the people of the land'. Verses 3–14 have been worked over
after the event, especially verse 14.

Chapter xvi. The use of the second person suggests direct
speech to Jerusalem.

Chapter xvii. The chapter shews first-hand knowledge of the
time of Zedekiah and seems to belong to about 588 B.C.

Verses 9b, 10, 16–18 seem to be glosses. The way in which Babylon is referred to does not seem to fit with its composition in Babylonia.

Chapter xviii. The three examples seem to refer to Josiah (5–9), Jehoiakim (10–13) and Zedekiah (14–20). The situation is pre-exilic.

Chapter xx. The references to Topheth (31) and to Canaanitish worship ('wood and stone') (32) point to Jerusalem as the scene of the prophecy.

Chapter xxi. 1–5 (= LXX and E.V. xx. 45–49). The prophet can only look on Teman and the Negeb, if in Palestine. Verse 12 (7) 'the tidings' seems to mean the three terrible prophecies of evil which we find in verses 2–4 (= xx. 46–48), 7–10 (= xxi. 2–5), 13–21 (= xxi. 8–16), 'it cometh', rather 'it has come' (בָּאָה).

Chapter xxiv. The Syriac and Vulgate omit a great part of verse 2 and read: 'Write thee the name of this day and utter a parable.' As we saw on p. 41, 'this selfsame day' points to a later insertion, but the insertion may have been by Ezekiel himself, introduced to elucidate the Text. The situation of the 'parable' seems to be Jerusalem itself.

Chapter xxxiii. According to xxiv. 25–27 the fugitive comes on the day of the Fall of Jerusalem. Here (verses 21–22) he comes half a year (or a year and a half) after, implying the Exile. But the exiles must have known such an event long before. The story is impossible. The reference to dumbness points back to iii. 26–27. The Editor seems to have understood this 'dumbness' to have lasted until the Fall of the City, but that is contrary to the whole Book. The dating reminds us of the hand responsible for i. 1 and viii. 1, and see xxxii. 17; xxxiii. 21 f. is therefore not genuine Ezekiel. xxiv. 25–27 seems closely linked with the preceding genuine passage (xxiv. 15–24), but the three times repeated בַּיּוֹם awakens doubts. The first is good sense. The second and third seem to be glosses (note the stylistically objectionable אֶת־הַפְּלִיט). In verse 27 the Editor introduces the idea of dumbness, which has nothing to do with 25–26. Either Ezekiel had withdrawn from Jerusalem to a place close by, or his house was in the inner part of the city. In either case the news is brought the same day.

Chapter xxxvii. 1–14. The valley of dry bones. The vision is Ezekiel's. 12–13 is an exilic addition, varying the picture. In verse 1 the Editor added 'in the spirit of Jehovah'; for 1a cf. iii. 22. Many fights may have taken place in the valley-plain, and Ezekiel, seeing the bones lying unburied, built upon them his prophetic symbolic vision. xxxvii. 15–19, a symbolic act, like those in iv and v. Apart from glosses (20, 26b and 28b) the whole section, although 21 ff. is an exilic appendix, is in the style of Ezekiel (cf. verse 16 'take thee' with iv. 1). If it is Ezekiel's, it is interesting to realize that he thought of a uniting of the two Kingdoms. Herntrich thinks that having lived through the Josianic Reformation, which extended to part of the Northern Kingdom, Ezekiel may have used 'the house of Israel' in an inclusive sense and have looked forward to a future United Kingdom.

To sum up: (1) The main body of the prophecies bear all the marks of delivery in person to the people in their own land, and it is possible to separate from them the passages which attribute them to a prophet living in exile in Babylon,* who may or may not be Ezekiel himself. (2) The vision of i. 4–28b with the latter references to it and certain characteristic phrases (as in xl. 1–3) are further clues which serve to distinguish the later exilic Editor's work from the original pre-exilic prophet.

---

* Prof. E. W. Barnes has written an article in the April number of the *J.T.S.* (1935) which puts forward arguments in favour of the traditional Babylonian sphere of origin, but he leaves untouched the positive arguments for the original delivery of the earlier prophecies in Palestine, as briefly set forth on pp. 23–25 and 58–60.

CHAPTER IX

THE LAST NINE CHAPTERS

We have made brief reference to the way in which these
chapters have been regarded by Herrmann and Hölscher
(p. 20) and by Herntrich (p. 30). We must now enter more
fully upon the problem raised by these chapters and come to
a decision as to its solution.

1. It is a matter of common agreement to-day that these
chapters form a complicated structure, which has only arrived
at its present form as the result of a gradual process. A number
of paragraphs have no logical connection with what precedes.
See for example xliii. 13 and 18, xliv. 1, xlv. 1, 9, 18, etc.
Herrmann and Hölscher are clearly right in finding the key
to the original conception in xl. 4 and xliv. 5. The prophet is
taken on a conducted tour through the Temple-to-be by 'a
man' with a line and a measuring reed in his hand. He is to
'behold' and 'hear' and 'set his heart upon' all that is shewn
to him and then he is to 'declare' it all to the house of Israel.
xliv. 5 follows up the earlier command by requiring the prophet
to hear and to declare the ordinances and laws, which are to
regulate the worship within the house. In xlvii. 1 the phrase
'he brought me' occurs for the last time. xlvii. 13–xlviii. 35
clearly fall outside the framework of the original version, and
large parts of xliii. 1 to xlvi. 18 are really later interpolations,
as may be seen by their contents, by the use of different
introductory formulae, such as 'Thus saith the Lord Jehovah'
(xliii. 18, xliv. 6, 9, xlv. 18, xlvi. 1, 16, xlvii. 13) and the closing
formula, 'Saith the Lord Jehovah' (xliii. 19, 27, xliv. 12, 15, 27,
xlv. 9, 15, xlvii. 23, xlviii. 29), and by contradictions.

The most complicated part is perhaps chapters xlv–xlvi.
This part therefore we will take as a sample of the rest.

xlv. 1–8 commands the distribution of a part of the land as a 'holy oblation' between the Priests, the Levites, the City and the Prince. xlii. 20 says that the Temple wall (500 cubits square) is to be the boundary between the holy and the common, but xlv. 1–5 declares that a portion, 25,000 by 20,000 square cubits, is to be holy. The latter must be by another hand. xliv. 28 says that the Priests have no inheritance in the land, but xlv. 4 assigns to them a definite portion. xlv. 1–8 clearly bases itself on xlviii. 1–8, 23–29 with its measuring of the areas of the twelve tribes. xlv. 8b passes into direct speech of Jehovah ('my princes...my people'). Probably this is intended to connect the paragraph with that which follows. Herrmann concludes from the use of 'let it suffice you' that xlv. 9ff. comes from the same hand as xliv. 6, and he explains the fact that the verses following xlv. 9 do not continue the subject of the 'princes' by the suggestion that a piece of the original must have been removed and also that the wording has been changed! When at last the duties of the prince in regard to the worship are mentioned, instead of the address to 'ye princes' we find xlv. 16f., 22–25, xlvi. 2–12. 'the prince' in the singular and in the third person. xlv. 10–12 seems (with Steuernagel and Hölscher) to be a marginal note to xlv. 13ff. xlv. 16 says that the tax of verses 13–15 is to be paid to the prince, from which he is to defray the cost of the sacrifices (xlv. 17). But it is generally agreed that the oblation was originally to be paid to the Priests (xliv. 30). 'You' in xlv. 13 is not now as in 9 'the princes', but the people, as xliv. 30a (though probably by a different hand). xlv. 17b is clearly a gloss and assumes xlvi. 2–12. xlv. 21a–24 gives regulations for the Passover. There seem here to be corrections made in order to bring the Text into conformity with the late P legislation of Num. xxviii. 16ff. 'Upon that day' in verse 22 does not refer to the 'seven days' of 21b, but to the first day of the

Feast, implied in 21 a. The Festival celebrations in every case are centralized as in Deuteronomy. xlv. 18–20 come from another hand, and deal with two atonements of the Sanctuary, on the first day of the first month and the first day of the seventh month. So the LXX, as in the margin of the Revised Version of verse 20. The MT has been corrected to make the verse conform to Lev. xvi, which deals with the great Atonement day on the tenth day of the seventh month. Both in xlv. 18 and 20 and in the similar passage xlvi. 13–15 the address is in the second person singular ('thou'). It seems to be taken from a P law-passage in which 'thou' is used (cf. Lev. ii. 4, etc., xxiv. 5, xxv. 8, etc.). In both passages 'the prince' is never mentioned. xlvi. 1–3, 8–10, 12 link on closely to xliv. 1–3 both by form and contents. xlvi. 16–18 and 19–24 do not seem to fit their present position. The later seems to be an addition which attaches itself to the original vision (? after xlii. 14).

2. If the reasoning in Chapter VIII (pp. 54 ff.) is accepted, the author of chapters xl–xlii can be identified with certainty. He is not the pre-exilic and early exilic prophet Ezekiel, but the subsequent Babylonian Editor, who added the vision of i. 4–28, etc. to the original call in chapters i–iii. By the dating in xl. 1 he shews himself to be the author of xxxiii. 21 (p. 59). 'In the visions of God' and 'appearance' (xl. 2–3) link on to i. 1–5. We find ourselves in these chapters in a world of thought in which the Temple worship is the absorbing topic. We note many links with the Levitical law of holiness. The old ideal of the future outlined in chapters xxxiv–xxxvii is forgotten or ignored. Volz and Mowinckel argue for a school of prophets as concerned in the elaboration of the cult-regulations. 'The man' of xl. 3, etc. is not Jehovah (as Jahn and Herrmann), who only takes Ezekiel (according to the author of xl. 1, 2) to Jerusalem (cf. viii. 3). Rather (with Hölscher and Herntrich) he is an angelic being, such as we frequently find in subsequent

post-exilic literature (Zechariah, Daniel, Enoch, etc.). Such an intermediate link between God and man is foreign to the genuine Ezekiel. Herrmann and Kittel think that the two different outlooks of xl ff. and i–xxxix can have belonged to one and the same man, but in spite of the interval of time such a transformation seems impossible. For example, the Messiah in chapters xxxiv–xxxvii is an ideal figure (cf. xvii. 22–24), a David redivivus (xxxiv. 23, xxxvii. 24), who will feed the flock in the future days, when Jehovah brings them back to their own land. 'The prince' of xliv. 3–xlvi. 18 is quite another figure. He is an actual member of an actual body of people, the secular head, as Hölscher says, of the congregation of the second Temple, alongside the spiritual head. Such was Shesh-bazzar, the 'prince' of Ezra i. 8. The author of P places such a 'prince' at the head of each of the twelve tribes (Num. ii. 3, 5, 7, etc., A.V. captain, R.V. prince; cf. Exod. xvi. 22, etc., Lev. iv. 22 translated 'rulers'). Rehoboam in 1 Kings xi. 34 is called נָשִׂיא, as being prince of a single tribe. In the Elephantine papyri mention is made of Ostanes alongside the High Priest and the Council of Elders. He appears to be the secular chief of the Jews in Jerusalem, and answers to the 'prince' of the later portions of Ezekiel xl–xlviii.

The latter plays an important part in the Temple worship, providing the sacrifices at the Feasts, the New Moons and the Sabbaths (xlv. 17–xlvi. 7) and enjoys honourable privileges (xliv. 3, xlvi. 2–12). These regulations seem to be older than the passages in P, where the princes of the tribes seem to be confined to regulating the secular affairs of the congregation, alongside Moses and Aaron, or Eleazar and Phinehas. The 'prince' passages in Ezekiel seem to belong to the fifth or late sixth centuries B.C. The High Priest does not find a place in Ezekiel xl–xlviii. Herntrich would place the passages about the prince between 535–521 B.C.

NOTE ON 'THE PRINCE'

נָשִׂיא occurs thirty-seven times in Ezekiel. Eight times it is used of foreign rulers (xxvi. 16, xxvii. 21, xxx. 13, xxxii. 29, xxxviii. 2, 3, xxxix. 1, 18), four times of the ruler of the Southern Kingdom (vii. 27, xii. 10, 12, xxi. 30 (25)), five times of princes of Israel (Judah) (xix. 1, xxi. 17 (12), xxii. 6, xlv. 8, 9), twice of Messianic David (xxxiv. 27, xxxvii. 25), eighteen times of the prince of xliv. 3–xlviii. 22. [On the other hand מֶלֶךְ occurs thirty-seven times, twenty times of foreign kings, twice of Jehoiachin (i. 2, xvii. 12), once of a king of Judah in general (vii. 27), three times of past kings of Judah (xliii. 7 bis, 9) and three of the future Messianic king (xxxvii. 22 bis, 24).] Herrmann thinks that Ezekiel rejects the hitherto royal dignity and only recognizes Jehoiakim as a prince (xxi. 30 (25)). But this will not bear examination. If Ezekiel will only give the inferior title to the last rulers of the Southern Kingdom, how does he come to give the same title to the ideal Ruler of the future Messianic Kingdom? As a matter of fact 'king' is not uniformly evaded (i. 17, xvii. 12, vii. 27). It is a curious fact that there has been some deliberate alteration of the titles 'king' and 'prince' either in MT or LXX. In vii. 27 MT has 'the king' (הַמֶּלֶךְ) and 'the prince' וְנָשִׂיא, but LXX B ἄρχων καὶ αἱ χεῖρες, A ὁ βασιλεὺς καὶ ὁ ἄρχων...καὶ αἱ χεῖρες. xxviii. 12 MT 'the king of Tyre', but LXX BA τὸν ἄρχοντα Τύρου. xxxvii. 22 MT 'king' twice, but LXX καὶ ἄρχων and omits the second. xxxvii. 24 MT 'king', but LXX ἄρχων. xxxii. 29 MT 'Edom her kings and all her princes', LXX οἱ ἄρχοντες Ἀσσούρ. In the next verse LXX translates נְסִיכֵי by the same οἱ ἄρχοντες. Herntrich says that MT adds 'and the prince' in vii. 27, while LXX strikes out the original 'king' and keeps only 'prince'; in xxxvii. 24 LXX substitutes 'prince' for original 'king' and in xxxii. 29 MT adds 'and all her princes', while LXX strikes

out the original 'kings' and only translates 'princes'. If, however, as we shall see in Chapter x and Excursus II, B in many
passages and phrases seems to present an earlier stage of the
Hebrew Text, it is questionable whether the present MT does
present us with the original Text. If not, then Herntrich's
attempt to prove that in the LXX we can observe a tendency
to weed out מלך in favour of נשיא falls to the ground. It is
noticeable that in chapters xl–xlviii clear evidence of a third
translator of the Book is to be seen in the ὁ ἀφηγούμενος (once
xliv. 3 ἡγούμενος), which in these chapters is the regular
LXX translation of נשיא. Herntrich makes an ingenious suggestion as to how נשיא came to be substituted for מלך in the
earlier chapters of Ezekiel i–xxxix. He puts together Jer.
xxiii. 33 and Ezek. xii. 10. In Jer. xxiii. 33, when the people
ask: What is the burden of Jehovah? the answer is given
(according to LXX and Latin): 'Ye are the burden, I will
cast you off, saith Jehovah.' In Ezek. xii. 10 the prophet
answers the same question by a pun: הַנָּשִׂיא הַמַּשָּׂא הַזֶּה, i.e.
'The prince is the burden'. This pithy expression has, he
says, unfortunately fallen into a wrong context. But it and
xxi. 30 has led to further use of 'prince' in place of 'king',
a tendency which was not Ezekiel's own purpose. But ingenious
as the suggestion is, it is too precarious to form a solid
foundation.

CHAPTER X

THE DOUBLE DIVINE NAME IN THE BOOK,
AS NOW PRESENTED IN THE MT

In the preceding chapters we have dealt with the literary
features of the Book of Ezekiel and have seen reason to think
that intermingled with the genuine work of Ezekiel we have
considerable passages which have been added by one or more
later writers. In this chapter we come to deal with a still more
fundamental question. Is there, alike in the original, and in
the later additional prophecies and narratives, an Editorial
activity, which has been consistently carried through in the
whole course of the Book? We noted at the outset (p. 3 f.) that
the double Divine Name אדני יהוה occurs 217 times in the
Hebrew Text of Ezekiel, whereas in the whole of the rest of
the Old Testament it occurs only 78 times. This unique
characteristic of the Book distinguishes it from any other of
the Prophetical Books, and until lately it has been attributed
to Ezekiel himself. The consistency with which certain simple
rules of phraseology in regard to the use of the Divine Name
are carried out in the present MT as compared with the
diversity and chaos of the usage found in the present state of
the LXX text seemed to point to the decisive superiority of
the MT, but recent studies have pointed to a different conclusion. It would seem that the consistent usage of the present
Hebrew Text is due to an Editor of much later date, possibly
about 100 B.C., and that the 'tossing about' of the Divine
Names in the LXX is due to Editorial changes in the Hebrew
Text and to the efforts of successive transcribers of the Greek
Text to bring it into conformity with the edited Hebrew Text.

It may seem at first sight as though that conclusion took

away from the value of the Book, but in reality it is not so. As we saw at the outset 'the spiritual value of the Book...is in no wise affected, except for good, by the reverent study of its structure from what we may call its architectural side'. We may gratefully welcome the Editorial action which gave additional solemnity to the prophetic message by duplicating the Divine Name in the two formulae with which so many of the prophecies were introduced and concluded.

Further, it has hitherto been taken for granted that the pronunciation of יהוה as אדני in the public reading of the Scriptures came first and that κύριος in the LXX was the natural translation of that usage. But it is very doubtful whether that pronunciation came in before 100 B.C., and, if that be the case, κύριος must have come in already independently in the LXX, seeing that this was translated about the third century B.C. The motive for the adoption of the word κύριος may well be traced to the feeling that merely to transliterate the sacred name (assuming that they knew its proper pronunciation) would have suggested that their God was merely one among other Gods. And a similar motive may well have led Palestinian revisers of the Hebrew Text to adopt אדני as the spoken substitute for יהוה in the public reading of the synagogue, and the written use of אדני would naturally follow. The whole question is a very complicated one, and, in order to deal with it adequately, the discussion has had to be relegated to an Appendix (Excursus II). To this the reader is referred. It is hoped that the facts will be carefully studied and it is believed that the conclusions given above will be recognized as sound.

Conclusion

If this be accepted as in line with all that has gone before, we may see an evolution of the Book of Ezekiel in Hebrew and in Greek somewhat as follows:

1. (a) An original Hebrew Text with single ᵉ throughout chapters i–xxxix, in which original prophecies of Ezekiel were put together, without careful chronological sequence, together with later prophecies of his own, by a disciple of the older prophet; and

(b) A corresponding Greek Text with single κύριος.

2. (a) A revision of the Hebrew Text with the addition of אֲדֹנָי to the original יהוה in certain phrases in which God speaks.

(b) The second part of the LXX Text (chapters xxi–xxxix) worked over by a Reviser, who introduced κύριος κύριος into many passages in accordance with the revised Hebrew Text. He or another afterwards introduced κύριος κύριος into chapters i–xx, which may at first have existed separately from chapters xxi–xxxix.

3. Later on, in the LXX, ἀδωναὶ κύριος, as witnessed to by many Lucianic MSS., seems to have become the favourite translation of ᵉ 'א and was inserted in passages where MT had ᵉ 'א, if κύριος κύριος was not already in position. Thus in our present LXX Text we see a mixture of the Original with later Edited Texts. This is specially seen in A and Q.

4. In chapters xl–xlviii (written at a later date) we see:

(a) A Hebrew exemplar, in which ᵉ 'א was used seventeen times.

(b) The original Greek translator had this Text and translated it by κύριος ὁ θεός. This part stands distinctly apart from the other two, both as to Text used and as to mode of translation. Κύριος κύριος seems to reflect the earlier pronunciation 'א 'א, while κύριος ὁ θεός reflects the pronunciation 'א, אלהים, which is stereotyped in the MT. This pronunciation, judging from the Old Latin, is pre-Hexaplaric.

CHAPTER XI

THE SPIRITUAL VALUE OF THE
BOOK OF EZEKIEL

The preceding studies have dealt exclusively with the literary
structure of the Book. A final word must be added, which
will briefly indicate the spiritual message which it enshrines.
It will be brief. For fuller treatment the reader is referred to
the Introductions which are to be found in the Commentaries
by Davidson, Skinner, and others.

If in the previous studies we have come to a right decision,
the Book presents to us the result of a remarkable partnership.
It is not the work of one man, still less was it produced in one
sustained effort at one time. There are two main authors and
it has received additions by later hands. The first author was
a prophet living in or near Jerusalem during the last years
of the Southern Kingdom. He saw with his own eyes the
abominations which were perpetrated by 'the house of Israel'.
He beheld violence and slaughter in the city, idolatry and
strange rites in the Temple, evil practices upon the hills. It
grieves his very soul and, as he meditates thereon, he falls into
a trance and he sees a hand, holding out to him a roll and
spreading it out before him, and there was written thereon,
within and without, lamentations and mourning and woe.
He is bidden to eat the roll and to go, speak unto the house of
Israel, speak My words unto them. He is warned at the outset
that they will not hear. He will find himself surrounded as it
were with briars and thorns and will dwell among scorpions.
But Jehovah will make his forehead as an adamant harder
than flint. He not only utters burning words of warning and

reproof and condemnation, but he uses various symbolic actions in the hope that things seen may reach minds that were impervious to things spoken. In chapter iv he takes a tile and portrays upon it a city and builds forts against it; he lies upon his side for three hundred and ninety days, representing the duration of the coming siege, and eats and drinks a daily ration of bread and water, measured strictly by weight and measure. In chapter v he takes a sharp knife, shaves off the hair of head and beard and burns and smites with the sword and scatters it to the wind. In chapter xii he ostentatiously makes a bundle of necessaries and goes forth with it from his house, as though he were going into captivity. In chapter xxiv, when his wife dies, he is bidden to exhibit no signs of mourning. Moreover, he is fond of allegories and parables—in chapter xv the vine, in xvii the two eagles, in xix the lioness and her cubs, in xvi and xxiii the harlot and the two wanton sisters. To him we probably owe not only the denunciations of the earlier chapters, but prophecies of Restoration (xxxiv–xxxvii) spoken in Captivity.

There is a second man of prophetic soul, who belongs to the period of the Captivity and who dwells in Babylonia. He may have been a young disciple of the older man and he imbibed much of his spirit. He may well have treasured up the recorded utterances of his Master and woven them in with his own oracles to form the first edition at least of the Book as we now have it. The glory of the God of Israel is that which overmasters his soul. The vision of the throne-chariot in chapter i is his. His is the conviction that Jehovah cannot dwell in the midst of a people so unworthy and rebellious or occupy any longer a Temple defiled by such idolatries and sins. He therefore pictures the glory of Jehovah, enthroned upon the chariot and the living creatures, departing from the Temple and from the city and passing away to the East. He is 'the priest in

the prophet's mantle' of whom Wellhausen spoke. He it is
who depicts the ideal Temple of the future and describes the
ordinances thereof, and who then tells how the glory of
Jehovah comes back to the building, which is henceforth to
be inalienably holy (xliii. 1–5, xliv. 2–4). Probably we owe
also to him the picture of the river of the water of life (chapter
xlvii) and the description of the ideal holy land, parcelled
out among the tribes.

But while we can with much probability assign certain
portions of the Book to one or other of these two prophetic
souls, yet the outstanding wonder of this Book of composite
authorship is the unity of the spiritual message which it presents. The two men are essentially one at heart, though each
has his own method of expressing the message. If, as we
believe, it is the second author to whom in the main we owe
the symmetry of the Book, we feel that he is able to do this,
because he has so assimilated the messages and writings of the
earlier prophet that they have become part of his own inner
mind and life.

The resultant message of the Book may be briefly summarized
as follows:

1. The first and overwhelming message, which dominates
the whole, is the inconceivable greatness of Jehovah, the God
of Israel. His omniscience and His omnipresence are shewn
in the description of the throne-chariot, its fourfold nature
(man, lion, ox, eagle), facing all ways and moving with equal
ease and celerity in all directions. His holiness and uniqueness
are emphasized over and over again and are made clear by
the elaborate provision against the coming near to the inner
shrine of the ideal Temple of anyone or anything that could
defile. His righteousness is shewn in His judgments alike upon
the heathen nations and upon His own people in their rebellious
ways. But also His mercy and loving-kindness are to be seen

in the restoration of His people to their renovated land, when they repent and abhor their past ingratitude and iniquity. Alike by His severity and by His loving-kindness towards Israel, the nations will learn to know 'that I am Jehovah'.

2. A new emphasis is laid upon a side of the Divine Nature, which has not hitherto been made prominent, viz. the energy of the Spirit. And this in two respects:

(i) The Spirit enters into the prophet and sets him on his feet (ii. 2), lifts him up and takes him away and speaks with him (iii. 12, 14, 24), lifts him up between the earth and the heaven and brings him in the visions of God to Jerusalem (viii. 3), lifts him up and brings him to the east gate of Jehovah's house, falls upon him and bids him speak (xi. 1, 5) and finally lifts him up and brings him back to Chaldea (xi. 24). The Spirit again takes action in chapter xxxvii. 1, carrying the prophet out into the midst of the valley of dry bones, and in chapter xliii. 5, where He takes him up and brings him into the inner court of the Temple. See also i. 12, 19, 20 and x. 17.

(ii) Chapter xxxvii brings home to us the second aspect of the Spirit's activity. The prophet is bidden to prophesy to הָרוּחַ and say: 'From the four רוּחוֹת come O הָרוּחַ, and breathe upon these slain that they may live.' הָרוּחַ came upon them and they lived (verses 9–10), and in verse 14 we read: 'I will put my רוּחַ in you and ye shall live.' It is this aspect of the Spirit's working which is brought out in xi. 19, xviii. 31, xxxvi. 26: 'A new heart will I give you and a new Spirit will I put within you....And I will put my Spirit within you and cause you to walk in my statutes.' It is in this respect that the Book most nearly anticipates the teaching of the New Testament.

3. It is often said that Ezekiel by his teaching in chapter xviii —that Jehovah deals with individuals according to their indi-

vidual merits or demerits—is declaring a new doctrine, as opposed to the old doctrine of the solidarity of the generations one with another, but that does not seem to be the true interpretation of the chapter. The prophet is opposing the outcry of 'the house of Israel' against Jehovah's treatment of them: 'The fathers have eaten sour grapes and the children's teeth are set on edge.' In other words they said: We of the present generation are quite innocent of evildoing on our own part (cf. p. 48 and 2 Kings xxiii. 26–27, xxiv. 3); we are suffering for our fathers' sins. The prophet upholds, not a new doctrine, but the old teaching of the righteousness of God, which deals with each man according to his works. 'The soul that sinneth, it shall die' (cf. Jer. xxxi. 29–30). There is an element of ideality in Ezekiel's treatment of this point. It cannot really be said that in the present scheme of things results are always proportionate to the actual merits or demerits of the individual soul.

4. The favourite image under which this Book speaks of the evildoing of 'the house of Israel' is that of whoredom (see chapters xvi and xxiii). This wantonness shewed itself in two directions:

(i) In their worship of false gods. Much at least of the worship in the high places was professedly Jehovah-worship, but it was so tainted by the use of images, as seen in the calves at Bethel, and by the heathenish immoralities which accompanied it, that Ezekiel, in common with Hosea (ii. 8–17) and Jeremiah (ii. 23–28), could only condemn it as offered really to Baal and not to Jehovah. Moreover, Israel carried on the abominable evil of child-sacrifice in the valley of Hinnom, slaying their children to their idols and then coming the same day into Jehovah's sanctuary to defile it (xxiii. 39).

(ii) In their political alliances with the heathen nations around (xxiii *passim*), instead of trusting in the living God and continuing faithfully in His ways. Even in Egypt they had allied themselves with idolators and in after days had 'doted' upon the Assyrians and Babylonians.

5. Yet Jehovah could not forget His people or utterly cast them away. 'Why will ye die, O house of Israel? For I have no pleasure in the death of him that dieth, saith the Lord God; wherefore turn yourselves and live' (xviii. 31 f.). Jehovah sends 'watchmen' to warn His people. If the wicked man will turn and do that which is lawful and right, he shall live thereby (xxxiii. 1–20). When they have gone into exile, yet for His own holy Name's sake Jehovah 'will take them from among the nations and bring them into their own land and will bless the corn and the wine and the waste cities will once more be filled with men' (xxxvi, especially 24–38). The two nations shall become one and David shall be their king (xxxvii. 15–28). This shall be, because they have received a new heart and a new Spirit.

6. Finally a vision is given of a new Jerusalem, glorified by a pure and holy Temple, wherein prince and people will offer acceptable service, and of a new land, ideally portioned out among the twelve tribes, and the name of the city from that day shall be, Jehovah-shammah, 'the Lord is there' (chapters xl–xlviii). The prophet of the Old Covenant rose to a great height of inspiration in his picture of the future. It was reserved for the seer of the Apocalypse to see a still greater vision—the Holy City, New Jerusalem, having the glory of God, coming down out of heaven from God and set up on earth. But there was one most significant change—'I saw no Temple therein, for the Lord God the Almighty, and the Lamb, are the Temple thereof.'

Excursus I

'THE HOUSE OF ISRAEL'

I. Amos

The earliest use of this phrase in prophetic literature is in the Book of Amos (v. 1, 3, 4, 25, vi. 1, 14, vii. 10, ix. 9).

The scene of his activity was the Northern Kingdom and in his prophecies 'the house of Israel' clearly had primary reference to that Kingdom (e.g. vii. 10). Some of the parallel expressions point to the same conclusion, especially 'the house of Joseph' (v. 6), 'the remnant of Joseph' (v. 15) and 'the affliction of Joseph' (vi. 6).

But there are other passages which suggest that the phrase did not exclusively in every passage mean the Northern Kingdom. On the contrary in iii. 1, where the cognate expression 'children (sons) of Israel', is used, the prophet says: 'Hear this word which Jehovah hath spoken against you, O children of Israel, against the whole family which I brought up out of the land of Egypt, saying: You only have I known of all the families of the earth.' The immediately preceding historical retrospect of ii. 9 ff., while it is the continuation of the paragraph dealing with Israel (verse 6) as distinguished from Judah (verse 4) (if ii. 4–5 be accepted as genuine), refers to events which were common to all 'the children of Israel' (verse 11). The combination of Bethel and Gilgal ('the circle') and Beersheba (v. 5) seems to include the South as well as the North. See also 'the way of Beersheba (query read "thy patron-saint, O Beersheba") liveth' (viii. 14), where its association with 'thy God, O Dan, liveth' in the same verse reminds us of the familiar phrase 'from Dan to Beersheba' (Judges xx. 1, etc.).

The house of Jacob iii. 13, ix. 8, the house of Isaac vii. 16, the high places of Isaac vii. 9, children of Israel ii. 11, iii. 1 (but LXX here reads 'house of Israel'), 12, iv. 5, ix. 7, Israel iv. 12 bis, vii. 9, 10, 16, ix. 7, My people Israel vii. 8, 15, viii. 2, ix. 14 seem to be used somewhat indiscriminately in the interests of poetic rhythm and to mean much the same in every case. The references to Zion vi. 1 and to 'the booth (סֻכַּת)', i.e. the dynasty 'of David', ix. 11, if by Amos, shew that Israel as a whole, and not the ten tribes only, are present in the prophet's mind.

II. HOSEA

Here we have again a prophet of the Northern Kingdom. If the possessive pronoun in vii. 5, 'our King', be trustworthy, he was himself a native of that Kingdom. His date was about 750 to 735 B.C.

'The House of Israel' only occurs four times in the Book. In i. 4 it is connected with 'the house of Jehu'. In v. 1 it is parallel in use to 'the priests' and to 'the house of the king'. Gesenius, Buhl and others understand the phrase in this context to stand for 'the authoritative representation of the people', but at any rate in vi. 10 and xii. 1 (xi. 12 in E.V.) it stands for the people of the Northern Kingdom as a whole. The more usual phrases in Hosea are Ephraim (37 times) and Israel (25 times) * in the present text, and in all probability originally also in xii. 3 (see next verse in the Hebrew) and v. 5–14. Israel is the name of the patriarch in xii. 12 (parallel to Jacob) and there probably is used to connect him with Israel the people, as referred to in the next verse. 'Children of Israel' occurs ii. 1, 2 (E.V. i. 10, 11), iii. 1, 4, 5, iv. 1 and nowhere else in

* iv. 15, 16, v. 3, 5 bis, 9, vi. 10, vii. 1, viii. 2, 3, 8, 14, ix. 1, 7, 10, x. 1, 6, 9, 15, xi. 1, 8, xiii. 1, 9, xiv. 1, 5.

the Book. This quite probably indicates the work of another writer. Samaria vii. 1, viii. 5 f., x. 5, 7, xiii. 16; Bethel, referred to by its proper name x. 15, xii. 4, but also under the nickname Bethaven, i.e. house of vanity, iv. 15, v. 8, x. 5; Gilead vi. 8, xii. 11; Gilgal iv. 15, ix. 15, xii. 12 (E.V. 11); Mizpah v. 1; Jezreel i. 4 f.; Shechem vi. 9; Tabor v. 1, all these belong to the Northern Kingdom and confirm the attribution of 'the house of Israel' in Hosea to the Northern Kingdom.

III. ISAIAH i–xxxix

The genuine passages date from 737 to (?) 701 B.C., but whole chapters are of exilic and post-exilic origin. As contrasted with Amos and Hosea, Isaiah is distinctively a prophet of the Southern Kingdom. The superscription is justified: 'The vision which Isaiah saw concerning Judah and Jerusalem.' At the same time there are prophecies against Northern Israel as well as against foreign nations.

'The House of Israel' occurs only three times. v. 7 'The vineyard of Jehovah of hosts is the house of Israel, and the men of Judah his pleasant plant'. Verse 3 and the parallelism in verse 7 identify the house of Israel with the men of Judah as one and the same people. viii. 14 The phrase 'both the houses of Israel' is unexampled, and the parallelism with 'the inhabitants of Jerusalem' points to the original reading as having been in the singular. xiv. 2 is in a clearly exilic passage (xiii. 1–xiv. 23) on Babylon. Its language corresponds to that of xlix. 22–23, lx. 4, 9–10.

The corresponding expression 'The house of Jacob' occurs in ii. 5–6, where verses 1–3 clearly connect the phrase with Judah, Zion and Jerusalem. viii. 17 is in a Zion-context. x. 20 The phrase 'the remnant of Israel' is parallel to 'the house of Jacob'. 'The remnant' (שאר) occurs also in verse 21 'the remnant of Jacob' and 22 'thy people Israel (or O Israel), a remnant shall return' and may have led to 20–23 (which is probably an exilic or post-exilic passage) being linked on to 19 'the remnant of the trees'. (שאר, we may note, occurs twelve times in Chron., Ezra, Neh., Esther, thirteen times in Isa. vii–xxviii, once in Zeph. i. 4 and once in Mal. ii. 15). 'Jacob' is frequently in parallel with Israel, as ix. 7 (E.V. 8). In the next verse we read: 'the people all of it shall know, even Ephraim and the inhabitant of Samaria', so that the reference here is clearly to the Northern Kingdom. In xiv. 1 Jacob (‖ Israel) is in the clearly exilic passage (xiii. 1–xiv. 23) on Babylon (see note on xiv. 2 above). xxvii. 6 'Jacob... Israel' is in a late post-exilic poem. xxix. 22 is regarded by Cheyne as a post-exilic insertion, and 'Jacob' and 'Israel' stand for the whole nation collectively. So does 'Israel' alone in i. 3–4, iv. 2, viii. 18, ix. 11 (E.V. 12), x. 17, 22, xi. 12. 'The mighty one of Israel' i. 24 and 'the Holy One of Israel' i. 4, v. 19, 24, x. 20, xii. 6, xvii. 7, xxix. 19, xxx. 11, 12, 15, xxxi. 1, xxxvii. 23 seem to regard the whole nation as one. But in xvii. 3 (though the Text seems to be in disorder) 'the children of Israel' seems to mean the Northern Kingdom (see Damascus, Syria and Ephraim in the context), while 'the children of Israel' for the undivided people in verse 9 is part of a later gloss (cf. xxvii. 12, xxxi. 6).

While therefore there are occasional uses of 'Israel' and 'Jacob' with special reference to the Northern Kingdom, no one of the three uses of 'the house of Israel' can be quoted as = the Northern Kingdom.

IV. MICAH

'The house of Israel' occurs three times in Micah, all three being in the chapters (i–iii) generally assigned to Micah.

i. 5a 'The sins of the house of Israel' is parallel to 'the transgression of Jacob'. The latter 'is it not Samaria?'

the former is Jerusalem and its high places. Samaria only is referred to in verses 6–8, Jerusalem comes in verses 9, 12, Zion in verse 13. Israel seems to mean the whole nation in verses 13–15.

iii. 1, 9c 'The rulers of the house of Israel' is parallel to 'ye heads of (the house of) Jacob'. Verse 8 seems to treat 'Jacob' and 'Israel' as two names for one and the same people. Verse 10 continues 'They build up Zion with blood and Jerusalem with iniquity', while no reference is made to Samaria or the Northern Kingdom (cf. verse 12).

Jacob in i. 5a, ii. 12, iii. 1 and 8, iv. 2 ('the house of the God of Jacob...for out of Zion shall go forth the law and the word of Jehovah from Jerusalem') is practically another name for Israel.

In iv. 14 (E.V. v. 1) 'the judge of Israel' and v. 1 (2) 'one that is to be ruler in Israel', 'Israel' may mean the land, for in v. 2 (3) the people are called 'the Sons of Israel'.

In vi. 2, 3 'Israel' is parallel to 'His people' and 'My people'. Here probably it stands for the undivided people, but if F. C. Burkitt's view be accepted that chapters vi and vii may be the work of a Northern prophet, then Israel may stand for the Northern Kingdom. It is therefore difficult to obtain from the Book of Micah a very clear idea as to the exact meaning of 'the house of Israel' as used therein.

V. Zephaniah

'The house of Israel' does not occur in Zephaniah, a Judaean prophet of the earlier years of Josiah. Israel definitely stands for Judah in iii. 13ff., where e.g. Israel is parallel to 'daughter of Zion'. 'The remnant of Israel' (iii. 13) means the same as 'the remnant of the house of Judah' (ii. 7), but iii. 15 'the King of Israel, even Jehovah' (cf. Isa. xliv. 6, xli. 21) seems to date from a period when there was no longer a king of the royal house upon the throne.

VI. JEREMIAH

'The house of Israel' occurs twenty times in Jeremiah, but the majority of these occurrences are in passages which are regarded as secondary (so e.g. A. S. Peake in his Commentary in the Century Bible).

We will first consider the twelve passages in which 'the house of Israel' seems to stand for Israel as a whole, including both North and South.

(i) ii. 4 'O house of Jacob and all the families of the house of Israel'.

(ii) ii. 26 'so is the house of Israel ashamed, they, their kings...'.

These two passages occur in the first group of discourses, spoken in the early years of Josiah, before 621 B.C. According to verses 2 and 28 the whole discourse is definitely addressed to Judah and Jerusalem. The LXX omits ii. 1–2a, but the καὶ εἶπεν without any indication as to who is the speaker is peculiar, and τῷ ἁγίῳ Ἰσραήλ, λέγει Κύριος is substituted for the last part of ii. 2. In verse 28 the LXX agrees with the MT in regarding the passage as addressed to Judah. The latter portion of verse 28 is also found in xi. 13 and the LXX adds here 'according to the number of the streets of Jerusalem they sacrifice to the Baal', which is practically the same as the LXX of xi. 13. It is obvious that the preceding verses are addressed to a people who are at the time worshipping stocks and stones.

If the whole passage is homogeneous, then Israel in verses 3 and 14 must at least include Judah. 'The house of Israel' in verse 26 is identified with the worshippers of idols, and the phrases in verse 4 are best understood as referring to the whole nation, no longer divided into two separate Kingdoms. 'All the families of the house of Israel' (ii. 4) may be compared with the phrase in xxxi. 1 (of later date) 'all the families of Israel' and must refer to Israel as a whole.

(iii) iii. 20 'as a wife treacherously departeth from her husband, so have ye departed treacherously from me, O house of Israel, saith Jehovah'. The third chapter does not seem to be homogeneous. In iii. 6–18 Israel is clearly the Northern Kingdom, as distinguished from Judah, but in the passages on either side 'Israel' is the Southern Kingdom, or the nation generally. Many therefore regard iii. 6–18 as an insertion here (even though it may be, in part at least, a later word of Jeremiah's). In that case iii. 19 follows immediately on iii. 5 and 'the house of Israel' is practically Judah and such Northern Israelites as are in connection with it. 'The children of Israel' in iii. 21 and 'Israel' in iii. 23, iv. 1 will have the same connotation. For verse 18 see the next section ((xiii), p. 86). If iv. 3 ff. were originally part of the same discourse, then the reference to Judah and Jerusalem is unmistakable (see verses 3–6, 10, 14, 16, 31), but the connection although probable cannot be regarded as certain.

(iv) and (v) v. 11 and 15 'the house of Israel and the house of Judah have dealt very treacherously against me...'; 15 'Lo, I will bring a nation upon you from afar, O house of Israel.' In verse 15 'the house of Israel' is clearly Judah. The people of the Northern Kingdom had been nearly a century in captivity and the threat of an invasion (15–16) which would eat up their harvest and beat down their fenced cities could not therefore apply to them. If v. 20 ff. belong to the same discourse, we have further evidence that the reference is to the Southern Kingdom. The words of verse 11, as they stand, clearly distinguish between 'the house of Israel' and 'the house of Judah', but the usage in verse 15 suggests that as usual the prophet meant by 'house of Israel' the same as in verse 15 and that a later Editor thought either that the phrase, as it stood, was ambiguous or that it meant the Northern Kingdom and therefore added 'and the house of Judah' and changed the verbs from singular to plural in order to include Judah.

(vi) ix. 25 (E.V. 26)' 'all the house of Israel are uncircumcised in heart' occurs in a detached oracle of two verses, which has no clear connection either with the preceding or the succeeding passages. There is mention of Egypt and Judah and Edom, etc., but no separate mention of the Northern tribes, and it may therefore be concluded that 'the house of Israel' stands either for the existing Kingdom of Judah, or for the whole people of Israel.

(vii) x. 1 'Hear ye the word..., O house of Israel'. The passage in which this occurs (x. 1–16) is apparently addressed to Israel in exile. The LXX omits verses 6–8 and places verse 9 between 5 a and 5 b. It has many features which recall Second Isaiah, and it is generally agreed that it is not by Jeremiah. Clearly 'the house of Israel' is not the ten tribes as distinguished from the two. It practically stands for Judah in exile.

(viii) and (ix) xviii. 6 'O house of Israel, cannot I do with you as this potter?...Behold as the clay..., so are ye in mine hand, O house of Israel'. The LXX omits the second 'house of Israel'. This occurs in a passage which is mainly by Jeremiah, but has been supplemented. Verse 11 definitely applies the message to the men of Judah and the inhabitants of Jerusalem, and verses 13, 17 speak of 'the virgin of Israel' as having 'done a very horrible thing', for which Jehovah will 'scatter (His people) as with an east wind before the enemy'. Clearly this is addressed to a people still in their own land and, if homogeneous with verse 6, shews that 'the house of Israel' there is Judah.

(x) xxiii. 7 'no more say, As Jehovah liveth, which brought up the children of Israel out of the land of Egypt, 8 but, As Jehovah liveth, which brought up...the seed of the house of Israel out of the north country...'. The LXX omits 'the house of', but in the parallel verse 7 it reads οἶκον for the MT 'children (sons)'. Moreover, the LXX puts verses 7–8 after verse 40. The same verses occur earlier in xvi. 14, 15, and there MT has 'children of Israel' in both verses and LXX has in verse 15 οἶκον 'Ισραήλ. For 'the seed (τὸ σπέρμα) of the house of Israel' comparison may be made with xxxi. 36 f., where the LXX twice renders 'the seed of Israel' by τὸ γένος 'Ισραήλ and the two verses are reversed in order. The hand of a second translator (xxix–li) is here revealed. It is not easy to decide whether verses 5–8 are, or are not, by Jeremiah. 'Shall reign as king' suggests a fairly early date. Judah and Israel in verse 6 seem to be used for the two Kingdoms, but they might be used as parallel synonyms and in xxxiii. 16, where the same passage is repeated, Jerusalem is substituted for Israel, as though they meant the same, but this may only reflect the opinion of the later writer.

(xi) xxxiii. 14 'Behold, the days come, saith Jehovah, that I will perform that good word which I have spoken concerning the house of Israel and concerning the house of Judah'. The whole passage (verses 14–26) is omitted in the LXX and was probably not in the Hebrew text before the translator. If so, it must be a very late addition. Verses 14–16 are virtually a repetition of xxiii. 5–6 (see (x)) but with addition of the words following 'saith Jehovah' in verse 14, the substitution of Jerusalem for Israel and the transference of the name: 'Jehovah is our righteousness', from the Messiah to the city. 'Shall reign as king' is no longer suitable and 'shall grow up unto David' is substituted. Verse 17 is not found in chapter xxiii and the expectation of an unbroken succession of Davidic kings and of a similar line of Levitical priests does not seem compatible with Jeremiah's authorship.

(xii) xxxiii. 17 'David shall never want...the throne of the house of Israel'. 'The house of Israel' here must at least include Judah, for the throne of David would naturally be in Jerusalem (as would also be the ministry of 'the priests the Levites', and see verse 16 'Judah' and 'Jerusalem'). It would therefore seem probable that the author of verse 14 belonged to a time when 'the house of Israel' was used of the ten tribes only and therefore he added 'and concerning the house of Judah' in order to include Judah in the good time coming. In the same way 'the two families' in verse 24 stand for Israel and Judah and are spoken of as 'my people' ('before *me*' should probably be read with some versions instead of 'before *them*' MT. Duhm would read 'before *him*').

It remains now to consider the passages in which we find 'the house of Israel' distinguished from 'the house of Judah'.

(xiii) iii. 18 'the house of Judah shall walk with the house of Israel'. See the discussion of the passage in (iii) (iii. 20) above (p. 83). Driver regards iii. 6–18 as genuinely Jeremiah's, but only inserted here later. Peake agrees with Driver in regarding iii. 6–13 as Jeremiah's, though inserted later, but regards iii. 14–15, 17–18 and 'when ye be multiplied and increased in the land in those days' (verse 16) as added by a later hand. Duhm regards only iii. 12b–13 as genuine, the rest of 6–18 being Editorial. Jeremiah, he says, in verse 12b meant by 'backsliding Israel' Judah, that being the only portion of the people of Israel which was still in their own land, but the later Editor took 'Israel' to mean the ten tribes. In verse 18 the two 'houses' are clearly distinct entities, but the expectation that they will return 'together' does not seem to agree with verses 11–13 and the prophecy seems to be exilic. v. 11, which, as it stands, treats the two 'houses' as distinct, has been discussed in (iv) and (v), where it is suggested that in verse 11 as in verse 15 Jeremiah spoke only of 'the house of Israel', meaning the existing Southern Kingdom, and that the later Editor either understood this as meaning the Northern Kingdom or as at the least ambiguous, and therefore added 'and the house of Judah' and altered the verbs accordingly.

(xiv) xi. 10 Here again, as it stands, 'the house of Israel' and 'the house of Judah' are spoken of as distinct, but verse 2 'speak unto the men of Judah and to the inhabitants of Jerusalem' and corresponding words in verses 6, 9, 12, 13 strongly favour the view that Jeremiah uses 'the house of Israel' as the name of the Southern Kingdom and that 'the house of Judah' is a later insertion by the Editor, to whom 'the house of Israel' meant the Northern Kingdom only.

(xv) xi. 17 'because of the evil of the house of Israel and of the house of Judah'. This verse comes under the same suspicion as xi. 10 and it is generally regarded as a later insertion by reason of its prosaic and conventional style.

(xvi) xiii. 11 'as the girdle..., so have I caused to cleave unto me the whole house of Israel and the whole house of Judah'. The context in verse 9 'will I mar the pride of Judah and the great pride of Jerusalem' and verse 13 'even the kings that sit upon David's throne...and all the inhabitants of Jerusalem' points to 'the whole house of Israel' as original and standing for the Southern Kingdom and 'the whole house of Judah' as added later.

(xvii) xxxi. 27 'I will sow the house of Israel and the house of Judah...'.

(xviii) xxxi. 31 'I will make a new covenant with the house of Israel and the house of Judah'.

(xix) xxxi. 33 'But this is the covenant...with the house of Israel...'.

Chapters xxx and xxxi seem to be a single, well-planned composition (and so Peake). The situation presumed in it, and the resemblances to parts of Second Isaiah, shew that in its present form it must be post-exilic, but certain passages seem to be genuinely Jeremiah's. The parallelism with chapter iii (in particular the invitation to Ephraim to return) is evidence for this, and the prophecy of the New Covenant almost certainly in its essence comes from Jeremiah himself. Verses 31 and 33 come in the last-mentioned passage. Verse 33 speaks only of 'the house of Israel'. By this phrase Jeremiah in the majority of genuine passages means the whole Israelite nation, and so here. It therefore seems probable that also in verse 31 the original reading was only 'the house of Israel' and that the later compiler added 'and the house of Judah' (cf. v. 11, xi. 10, xiii. 11, xxxiii. 14). The elimination of the latter words restores the Qina Rhythm.

Verse 27 belongs to the preceding section 23–30. In the earlier part of the chapter Jeremiah refers to the Northern Kingdom (note 'Israel' 2, 9, virgin of Israel 4, 21, mountains of Samaria 5, the remnant of Israel 7, Ephraim 6, 9, 18, 20, Rachel and Ramah 15) and anticipates the return of its people. But verses 23–30 treat of the land of Judah and the cities thereof and 'the God of Israel' promises the return to them. When therefore we read in verse 27 of 'the house of Israel and the house of Judah' it is open to question whether the phrase is to be interpreted in the same way as verses 31, 33 or as a summing up by the later Editor of the whole passage 2–26. The fact that verse 27 begins 'Behold, the days come, saith Jehovah' as in xxx. 3 and xxxi. 31, 38 perhaps points to the second alternative, but in any case the phrase seems to belong to the later Editor.

(xxxiii. 14 is discussed under (xi).)

(xx) xlviii. 13 'the house of Israel was ashamed of Bethel

their confidence'. The whole chapter is of doubtful authorship, but there may be a nucleus of Jeremiah's words. The reference to Bethel (cf. Amos v. 4, 5 and note above, p. 77) points to 'the house of Israel' as the Northern Kingdom.

The final conclusion to which we come is that in the Book of Jeremiah 'the house of Israel' in ii. 4, 26, iii. 20, v. 15, ix. 25 (E.V. 26), x. 1, xviii. 6 (twice), ? xxiii. 8, xxxi. 33, xxxiii. 17 stands either for the Southern tribes or for the whole people. In iii. 18, v. 11, xi. 10, 17, xiii. 11, xxxi. 27, 31, xxxiii. 14, xlviii. 13 it would appear on the face of it to stand for the Northern Kingdom. But in v. 11, xi. 10, xiii. 11, xxxi. (? 27), 31, xxxiii. 14 the phrase may have originally stood for the whole people and the later Judaean Editor misunderstood this and added 'and the house of Judah'. The usage in the former group almost always occurs in genuine Jeremiah passages, and the usage in which it stands for the Northern tribes for the most part occurs in passages by a later hand.

VII. ISAIAH xl–lxvi

'The house of Israel' is only used twice. 'The house of Jacob' occurs three times. They are identical in meaning. 'House of Judah' is not found at all.

xlvi. 3 'Hearken unto me, O house of Jacob and all the remnant of the house of Israel'. The passage ends (verse 13 R.V.m.) 'I will give salvation in Zion and my glory unto Israel'. Here Israel and Zion are used as practically synonymous in meaning, and so are Jacob and Israel in verse 3. Cf. xlviii. 1 'Hear ye this, O house of Jacob, which are called by the name of Israel and are come forth out of the waters of Judah...' and xlviii. 2, 12, 20, xlix. 3, 5, 6, lviii. 1

lxiii. 7 'the great goodness toward the house of Israel'; cf. verse 17, lxiv. 10f. Israel, Jacob and the tribes are identified with Zion and its circle.

VIII. Zechariah i–viii

'The house of Israel' only occurs once—in a passage which is full of references to Zion and Jerusalem.

viii. 13 'as ye were a curse among the nations, O house of Judah and house of Israel, so will I save you... 14 As I thought to do evil unto you..., 15 so again have... to do good unto Jerusalem and to the house of Judah' (and see verses 3 f., 7 f., 19). It is possible that 7 'my people' may include members of the Northern Kingdom, but the whole number is not thought of as very numerous, for 'they shall dwell in the midst of Jerusalem' (verse 8) and the exhortation 'let your hands be strong' (verse 9) are in fact addressed to those who have already returned and especially to 'the house of Judah' (verses 15 and 19). It is noticeable that in verse 13 'O house of Judah' comes first and the only other reference to Israel is in ii. 2 (E.V. i. 19), where the Hebrew text suggests that it is an explanatory gloss. In ii. 4 (E.V. i. 21) Judah is twice mentioned alone, and it is probable that in viii. 13 'the house of Israel' is also Editorial.

IX. Zechariah ix–xiv

The date of these chapters may be 332–300 B.C. (Knipe) or 306–278 B.C. (Stade, G. A. Smith) or second century (Kennett). 'The house of Israel' does not occur in these chapters. 'The house of Judah' occurs three times.

x. 3 'Jehovah hath visited his flock, the house of Judah'.

x. 6 'I will strengthen the house of Judah and I will save the house of Joseph and I will bring them again.... 7 Ephraim shall be like a mighty man.... 10 I will bring them into the land of Gilead and Lebanon'.

xii. 4 'I will open mine eyes upon the house of Judah'.

In x. 6 it will be noticed that 'the house of *Joseph*' is mentioned alongside 'the house of Judah', in verse 7 Ephraim is spoken of and in verse 10 Gilead and Lebanon. The author of this passage combines the people of the Northern Kingdom along with those of Judah.

This concludes the references to the house of Israel in the Later Prophets (Ezekiel excepted. See xii, below). We pass now to

X. The Former Prophets

Joshua xxi. 45 'There failed not...any good thing which Jehovah had spoken unto the house of Israel' (LXX τοῖς υἱοῖς Ἰσραήλ). This passage uses the phrase 'the house of Israel' in the same way as P in Exod.–Num. (see the next section).

1 Sam. vii. 2, 3 'all the house of Israel lamented after Jehovah', 'and Samuel spake unto all the house of Israel'. In the following verses the alternation between 'the children of Israel' and 'Israel' seems to point to the whole passage as being composite, verses 2–4, 6b, 7a, c, 8 coming from a prophetic narrative, using 'children of Israel' and here twice 'house of Israel' for the undivided Kingdom. Verses 7b, 9, 10a, b, 11, 13, 14a, b, c, 15, 16, 17 belong to a civilian narrative.*

2 Sam. i. 12 David and his men mourned 'for Saul...and for the people of Jehovah and for the house of Israel'. Wellhausen and Budde delete the last clause. Budde suggests that it may have been added in consequence of the erroneous reading 'Judah' in the LXX instead of 'Jehovah'.

vi. 5, 15 In both verses 'David and all the house of Israel'. The LXX in verse 5 has 'the children of Israel'. The passage comes from the prophetic source.

xii. 8 'I...gave thee the house of Israel and of Judah'. Verses 7b–8 and 10–12 are probably an insertion by a pro-

* See Sachsee, *The meaning of the name Israel.*

phetic hand. The words 'and of Judah' are suggestive of a writer in the days of the divided Kingdoms.

xvi. 3 Mephibosheth is reported by Ziba to have said: 'Now shall the house of Israel restore me the kingdom of my father.' 'The house of Israel' either points to the time when the ten tribes were so called or possibly it stands for 'the authoritative representation of the people', as may be the case in Hosea i. 4, 6 (see p. 78).

1 Kings xii. 21 'Rehoboam...assembled all the house of Judah and the tribe of Benjamin...to fight against the house of Israel'.

xx. 31 'the kings of the house of Israel are merciful kings'.

Both these passages naturally use the phrase for the ten tribes.

In the early chapters of 2 Samuel Israel is frequently used for the ten tribes under Ishbosheth (ii. 9, 10, 17, 28, iii. 10, 17, iv. 1), while 'the house of Judah' (ii. 4, 7, 10b, 11) is used for the tribes under David. But also 'Israel' is used of the whole nation (as in i. 19, 24, iii. 37f., v. 1-3, 12, 17, vi. 1, 5, 15, vii. 7, 8, 10f., 24, 27 (∥ 1 Chron. xvii. 22, 24), viii. 15, etc.

XI. THE PENTATEUCH

'The house of Israel' is only found in sections which are ascribed to the Priestly document.

Exod. xvi. 31 'The house of Israel (LXX οἱ υἱοὶ Ἰσραήλ) called the name thereof Manna'.

xl. 38 'The cloud of Jehovah was upon the tabernacle by day...in the sight of all the house of Israel' (LXX ἐναντίον παντὸς Ἰσραήλ).

Lev. x. 6 'Let your brethren, the whole house of Israel, bewail' (LXX πᾶς ὁ οἶκος Ἰσραήλ).

xvii. 3, 8, 10 'Whosoever there be of the house of Israel'

(LXX in all three verses translates ἄνθρωπος ἄνθρωπος τῶν υἱῶν Ἰσραήλ).

xxii. 18 'Whosoever there be of the house of Israel' (LXX ἄνθρωπος ἄνθρωπος ἀπὸ τῶν υἱῶν Ἰσραήλ).

Num. xx. 29 'all the congregation...mourned for Aaron, thirty days, all the house of Israel' (LXX πᾶς οἶκος Ἰσραήλ).

Five times the LXX reads 'children' for 'house', twice it agrees with MT; once it reads 'all'. In every case 'the house of Israel' is the whole body of Israelites. It is used in MT of the Pentateuch only these eight times, while 'the children of Israel' is used 300 times in P. The phrase is not used at all in JE or D. In Exod. xix. 3 we find 'the house of Jacob' used as parallel to 'the children of Israel'. This is probably by JE^D.

In Josh. xvii. 17 and Judges i. 22, 23, 35 the tribes of Ephraim and Manasseh are called 'the house of Joseph', while in Judges x. 9 we read of 'the house of Ephraim'. 'The children of Joseph' is found in Josh. xvii. 14, 16. These passages are to be attributed to J.

XII. EZEKIEL

We have kept to the last the study of the usage of 'the house of Israel' in Ezekiel. The phrase, as we have seen, occurs eighty-three times. These passages must be examined one by one and the indications, so far as they exist, as to the persons meant by the phrase must be observed in each case.

iii. 1–7 The prophet is sent to 'the house of Israel' (verses 1, 4, 5, 7 bis). They are 7 of a hard forehead, 9 a rebellious house. These characteristics point not to the exiles, but to the guilty inhabitants of Judah and Jerusalem (see Chapter IV, pp. 23–25).

iii. 17 Ezekiel is made 'a watchman unto the house of Israel'. There is no special indication here as to the persons to be warned.

iv. 3 'This shall be a sign unto the house of Israel'. The sign is a tile on which is portrayed a city, and an iron pan. 'Even Jerusalem' is probably a gloss. If the sign was actually performed in the city, there was no need to specify it more particularly. But 'the siege of Jerusalem' in verse 7 seems to be part of the original, and so also in verse 16 'the staff of bread in Jerusalem'.

iv. 4f. 'lie thou upon thy left side and lay the iniquity of the house of Israel upon it...so shalt thou bear the iniquity of the house of Israel'. It seems clear that a later hand has re-interpreted the duration of the siege as though it referred to the duration of the exile. He has taken 'the house of Israel' as meaning the Northern Kingdom and has added verse 6 with its 'forty days, each day for a year' and 'the house of Judah', and also verses 9b, 12–15, 17.

v. 4 'Therefrom shall a fire come forth into all the house of Israel'. This is a continuation of the signs in chapter iv. The prophet, verse 2, is to burn one third of his hair 'in the midst of the city according to the fulfilling of the days of the siege'. The sign is obviously spoken and acted in Jerusalem during the siege. Verses 3–4 may be an addition, but that does not affect the reference to Jerusalem. Verse 5 begins 'This is Jerusalem'—a true statement, though it is doubtfully due to Ezekiel himself, for verses 5–17 are probably by a later hand, who uses Ezekielian phrases and thoughts.

vi. 11 'Aha, because of all the evil abominations of the house of Israel'. Verses 11–14 may be a summary of the passionate protests of the prophet against the idol-altars on hill and under tree. 'From the wilderness to Riblah' (MT Diblah) seems to include the whole land from South to North. In verses 13, 14

the initial words 'Ye shall know that I am Jehovah' point
to the subsequent possessive pronouns as having been altered
from second to third person to suit the Babylonian theory.
The primary reference must be to Jerusalem and Judah, where
it seems clear that idol-worship went on in the last years before
the Final Exile, but it may well be that the remnant of the
Northern tribes continued their worship in the high places
(see Zech. vii. 2). 'The mountains of Israel' in verses 2 and 3
would naturally include the Northern hills.

viii. 6 'The great abominations that the house of Israel do
commit here that I should go far off from my sanctuary'.
Whether the visit to Jerusalem be in reality or in vision only,
the conclusion is the same, viz. that 'the house of Israel'
commit their abominations in the Temple at Jerusalem.

viii. 10–12 'all the idols of the house of Israel' are portrayed
upon the walls of the chamber and the elders of 'the house
of Israel' burn incense to them. It is a question whether
verses 16, 17, where the phrase is 'the house of Judah', is
part of the genuine Ezekiel.

ix. 9 'The iniquity of the house of Israel and Judah is
exceeding great'. (See Chapter VIII (p. 57 f.) for evidence that
chapters ix–x are by a later Editor.) Here in any case the
scene is Jerusalem and the Temple (verses 4–8). It is 'the
residue of Israel' which is being destroyed. The expression
'house of Israel and Judah' betrays a late hand. 'And Judah'
may have been added later.

xi. 5 'Thus have ye said, O house of Israel...'. 'Ye have
multiplied your slain in this city' (verse 6) points to Jerusalem
as still the scene, and so does the death of Pelatiah (verses 1
and 13). 'The remnant of Israel' (verse 13) are in Jerusalem
(as ix. 8).

xi. 15 'thy brethren...and all the house of Israel, all of
them, are they unto whom the inhabitants of Jerusalem have

said: Get you far from Jehovah'. 'The house of Israel' is here used for the exiles, but this is quite contradictory to viii. 6, 10–12, and the whole passage xi. 14–21 bears the marks of an independent and later writing.

xii. 6 'I have set thee for a sign unto the house of Israel'. 9 'the house of Israel, the rebellious house'. 10 'The prince in Jerusalem and all the house of Israel'. 24 'there shall be no more any vain vision...in the midst of the house of Israel'. 27 'Behold, they of the house of Israel...'. Textually the early part of the chapter is in disorder and has clearly been worked over by the Editor. 'I am your sign' (verse 11) and the pronouns in the second person in the Syriac text are specially noteworthy.

xii. 21–25 and 26–28 seem to be, both of them, genuine Ezekiel pieces and are good examples of the prophet's duplication of his messages. In any case our phrase in all five verses is only intelligible when seen to be the name for the people in Jerusalem.

xiii. 5, 9 'The prophets of Israel' (verse 2) 'have not...made up the fence for the house of Israel, to stand in the battle...'. Therefore 'they shall not be...written in the register of the house of Israel, neither shall they enter into the land of Israel'. The last words imply that the prophets are in exile (cf. xx. 38), but the whole passage seems late and verse 9 specially so. These 'prophets of Israel' in any case (verse 16) 'prophesy concerning Jerusalem' and not the Northern Kingdom.

xiv. 4–11 Our phrase is used in this passage five times. In verses 4 and 7 the same wording is used as in Lev. xvii. 3, 8, 10 'what man soever there be of the house of Israel (or of the strangers that sojourn in Israel)'. Verse 7 implies that the house of Israel are the people still in the land. 'Strangers that sojourn in Israel' would be unintelligible, if spoken of Babylonia. If verse 1 'the elders of Israel...sat before me' is trustworthy these men were men who came to Ezekiel's house in Jerusalem (see Chapter IV, p. 29).

xvii. 2 'Speak a parable unto the house of Israel.' The parable of the two great eagles refers to the fate of Jehoiachin and Zedekiah, and therefore the house of Israel are the people of the land of Judah.

xviii. 6, 15, 25, 29 bis, 30, 31 Verse 6 'the idols of the house of Israel', 15 'the idols of the house of Israel', 25 'O house of Israel, is not my way equal?', 29 'yet say the house of Israel...', 'O house of Israel, are not my ways equal', 30 'therefore I will judge you, O house of Israel', 31 'why will ye die, O house of Israel?'. The chapter deals with a saying current in (על, as Amos vii. 17, Isa. xiv. 2) the land of Israel (cf. verse 3 'in Israel'). The three examples are 5–9 Josiah, 10–13 Jehoiakim, 14–20 Zedekiah. The whole situation is that of Jerusalem in the last years before the capture of the city.

xx. 13, 27, 30, 31, 39, 40, 44 (verses 1 and 5 The elders of Israel come and sit before Ezekiel. 'In the day when I chose Israel and...the seed of the house of Jacob...in the land of Egypt'). 13 'But the house of Israel rebelled against me in the wilderness', 27 'Speak unto the house of Israel', 30 'Say unto the house of Israel...Do ye pollute yourselves...31 when ye make your sons to pass through the fire...unto this day? And shall I be inquired of by you, O house of Israel?', 39 'O house of Israel..., Go ye, serve everyone his idols... 40 for in mine holy mountain, in the mountain of the height of Israel..., there shall all the house of Israel, all of them, serve me in the land, 44 when I have wrought with you..., O ye house of Israel'. Verses 33–44 are an exilic prophecy of salvation. The reference to Topheth in verse 31 with 'unto this day', and to Canaanitish worship in 32 ('to serve wood and stone', cf. Jer. ii. 27), shews that the people spoken to were men of Jerusalem and Judah.

xxii. 18 (2 'judge the bloody city', 3 'a city...that maketh idols'). Verse 17 begins a new passage, 18 'the house of Israel is become dross unto me', 19 'therefore I will gather you into the midst of Jerusalem'. The second person 'you' is noteworthy. The audience are in and around Jerusalem.

xxiv. 21 (18 death of wife, but 17 no mourning). 21 'Speak unto the house of Israel:...I will profane my sanctuary... 22 and ye shall do as I have done....24 Ezekiel shall be to you a sign.' The situation is Jerusalem. Its people are the audience.

xxviii. 24–25 Verse 24 'no more a pricking brier unto the house of Israel...25 when I shall have gathered the house of Israel from the peoples...and they shall dwell in their own land which I gave to my servant Jacob'. The passage is exilic. The house of Israel is now in exile. 'The land' is Palestine generally.

xxix. 6, 16, 21 (Prophecy against Pharaoh). 6 Egypt has 'been a staff of reed to the house of Israel', 16 'it shall be no more the confidence of the house of Israel'. It was the Southern Kingdom, which had dealings with Egypt. 21 (seventeen years later) 'I will cause a horn to spring forth to the house of Israel'. This prophecy, if by Ezekiel, was delivered late in his career.

xxxiii. 7, 10, 11, 20 (Prophet as watchman, xxxiii. 1–9 = iii. 16–21). 7 'I have set thee a watchman to the house of Israel', 10 'say unto the house of Israel...11 for why will ye die, O house of Israel?' Verses 10–20 are a new paragraph and are parallel to chapter xviii. 10–11 = xviii. 31–32. Only if the prophet is in Jerusalem can he 'blow the trumpet' (verses 3, 6) so as to warn 'the people of the land', 20 'O house of Israel, I will judge you, everyone after his ways', so xviii. 30. The people are clearly still in their own land.

xxxiv. 30 (Prophecy 1–6, 17–22 against the evil shepherds

and 23–31 of the One Shepherd), 'they, the house of Israel, are my people'. Verses 25–31 may not be Ezekiel's, but in any case the house of Israel are the people whom Jehovah will restore to their own land. He 'will make them and the places round about my hill a blessing'. Compare verse 14 'upon the mountains of the height of Israel shall their fold be'. The prophet thinks of the whole original land of Israel as the future abode of the people of Jehovah.

xxxv. 15 Mt Seir and Edom are reproached, because 'thou didst rejoice over the inheritance of the house of Israel because it was desolate'. The whole people may here be thought of, but more probably the reference is to the Southern Kingdom.

xxxvi. 10, 17, 21, 22 bis, 32, 37 (Prophecy to the mountains of Israel). Israel is in exile. Enemies take possession of the land. 10 'I will multiply men upon you, all the house of Israel', 17 (new paragraph) 'When the house of Israel dwelt in their own land, they defiled it..., 19 and I scattered them', 21 'I had pity for my holy name, for the house of Israel had profaned it...22 Therefore say unto the house of Israel... I do not this for your sake, O house of Israel', 32 'Not for your sake...be ashamed..., O house of Israel', 37 'For this moreover will I be inquired of by the house of Israel'. The last verse of the chapter (xxxvi. 38) speaks of 'the flock of Jerusalem in her appointed feasts'. It may not be Ezekielian, but it shews that the writer's thought centred round Jerusalem. The earlier part of the chapter, with its rhetorical address to the mountains, must include the whole range of hills from North to South of Palestine.

xxxvii. 11, 16 (The vision of the dry bones). 11 'These bones are the whole house of Israel'. This would seem to envisage the twelve tribes as an ideal whole. Verses 15–19 tell of a symbolical act like those of chapters iv and v, followed by a later appendix (21 ff.). 15–19 may well be Ezekiel's.

16 'For Judah [and for the children of Israel his com-
panions]....For Joseph [the stick of Ephraim and all the
house (LXX υἱούς) of Israel his companions (cf. 19 and 21)]
17 and join them into one stick.' Hölscher deletes the words in
square brackets as glosses, the glossator regarding Judah and
Joseph as single tribes and therefore adding words to include
the other tribes. 'The children of Israel' in verse 21 probably
stands for the whole twelve tribes in idea (cf. xliii. 7, xliv. 9, 15,
xlvii. 22, xlviii. 11). (In ii. 3, iv. 13, vi. 5a, xxxv. 5 'the
children of Israel' seems to be Editorial. In three out of the
four passages the LXX differs from MT, reading 'children'
only in iv. 13.)

xxxix. 12, 22, 23, 25, 29 (The defeat of Gog). 12 'Seven
months shall the house of Israel be burying them'. (In verse 13
'all the people of the land'), 22 'the house of Israel shall
know that I am Jehovah their God...23 and the nations shall
know that the house of Israel went into captivity for their
iniquity'. 25 'Now will I bring again the captivity of Jacob
and have mercy upon the whole house of Israel...'. 29 'I have
poured out my spirit upon the house of Israel'. The restored
people seem to be regarded as the remnant of the whole
nation.

xl. 4 (Temple vision). 'declare all that thou seest to the
house of Israel'.

xliii. 7, 10 Verse 7 'my holy name shall the house of Israel
no more defile', 10 'shew the house to the house of Israel...'.

xliv. 6 bis, 12, 22 Verse 6 'Thou shalt say to the rebellious,
even to the house of Israel:...O ye house of Israel, let it suffice
you...', 12 (The idolatrous Levites) 'became a stumbling-
block...unto the house of Israel', 22 (The priests) 'shall take
for their wives...virgins of the seed of the house of Israel'.

xlv. 6, 8, 17 bis Verse 6 'The possession of the city', 'it shall
be for the whole house of Israel', 8 'my princes...shall give

the land to the house of Israel according to their tribes', 17 'In all the appointed feasts of the house of Israel...to make atonement for the house of Israel'. Cf. xlviii. 1–35, where each of the twelve tribes is assigned its portion of the land and its gate into the city.

Clearly in all these passages in chapters xl–xlviii the future people of Israel are regarded in ideal as the twelve tribes now happily reunited. Cf. Acts xxvi. 7.

The conclusion as to the meaning of 'the house of Israel' in Ezekiel has been summed up in Chapter v (pp. 31 f.).

THE DIVINE NAMES IN EZEKIEL

One of the outstanding textual problems presented by the Book of Ezekiel concerns the use of the double Divine name אדני יהוה in that Book.

Johannes Herrmann in·an essay: *Die Gottesnamen in Ezechiel-texte* (1913), sought to prove that Ezekiel's usage can be reduced to a few simple and easily intelligible rules and that with insignificant exceptions these rules are strictly observed in the Masoretic Text. His argument ran as follows:

(1) The double name is used only in three connections:

(*a*) in the introductory formula כה אמר א׳ י׳,*

(*b*) in the concluding formula נאם א׳ י׳, and

(*c*) in addressing the Almighty by name.

In the MT א׳ י׳ occurs 217 times and of these all but nine are found in one of the three connections just stated. In the formula (*a*) the double name occurs 122 times against four instances of כה אמר י׳. In the formula (*b*) we find 81 times the double name and only four times נאם י׳. Of (*c*) there are only five examples and no exceptions.

(2) יהוה (by itself) occurs 218 times and regularly in the following connections:

(*a*) in the phrase אני י׳ 87 times as against five examples of אני א׳ י׳,

(*b*) after a construct state (excluding נְאֻם) 94 times as against four exceptional occurrences of א׳ י׳ in this connection,

(*c*) י׳ also occurs 37 times in other connections.

The bare אדני is used only four times (Baer, etc., admit a

---

* Throughout this Excursus א׳ י׳ is used as short for אֲדֹנָי יַהְוֶה.

fifth time in xxi. 14) and that in a proverb quoted from the
mouth of the people (xviii. 25, 29, xxxiii. 17, 20). It is (says
Herrmann) impossible to resist the inference that Ezekiel's
own practice was regulated by the principles here indicated;
and that the few exceptions noted represent the amount of
error that has crept into the transmission of the Hebrew text.

Turning to the LXX text Herrmann finds that in its best
text (that of B) יהוה except in xx. 38 is invariably rendered
by κύριος: on the other hand א' י' is represented 58 times by
κύριος κύριος,* twice by ἀδωναί κύριος (but this may be a
Hexaplaric correction), 113 times by κύριος, seven times by
κύριος ὁ θεός and nine times by κύριος θεός.† A few LXX
variations comply with the rules given above and are therefore to be regarded as original, but it can be no longer main-
tained that the LXX is the better text, or that it rests on a
Hebrew basis differing from the MT.

This argument seemed conclusive at the time, but since then
Graf von Baudissin's voluminous work *Kyrios als Gottesname
im Judentum*, edited by Prof. Eissfeldt, has appeared. The first
two volumes present an exhaustive argument to prove that,
after all, the B text shews the way to the true original text
of the Book of Ezekiel, and we are compelled to ask: What if
the consistency with which certain simple rules of phraseology
are carried out in the MT is due not to the original author,
but to an Editor? What if the 'tossing about' of the Divine
names in the LXX is due to such Editorial changes in the
Hebrew text and to the efforts of successive transcribers of
the LXX text to bring it into conformity with the edited
Hebrew text?

This study is directed to the answering of these questions.

* 54 times B*, 3 times B^ab, once for יהוה alone (see Table VI,
p. 161).

† See Table IV, pp. 153 ff.

The first step must be to note carefully the actual facts of the position on either side.

I. Taking first the MT, we note

  1. The distribution of the double name in the whole O.T.

    In the Pentateuch we find 4 occurrences.*

    In the Former Prophets we find 11 occurrences.†

    In the Later Prophets we find 282 occurrences,‡ of which 217 are in Ezekiel.

    In the Kᵉthuvim we find 8,§ making a total of 305 (see Table I, p. 149).

It is clear at once that the double name is closely associated with the prophetical Scriptures.

But further we must note

  2. The *use* of the double Divine name in these Scriptures.

The four uses in the Pentateuch are all in the vocative in address to God.

Twice in Gen. xv. 2, 8. The passage appears to be an

---

* Gen. xv. 2, 8, Deut. iii. 24, ix. 26 (all four in vocative).

† Josh. vii. 7, Judges vi. 22, xvi. 28, 2 Sam. vii. 18, 19 bis, 20, 28, 29, 1 Kings viii. 53, ii. 26 (first 10 in vocative).

‡ Isaiah (25 times), iii. 15, vii. 7, x. 23, 24, xxii. 5, 12, 14, 15, xxv. 8, xxviii. 16, 22, xxx. 15, xl. 10, xlviii. 16, xlix. 22, l. 4, 5, 7, 9, lii. 4, lvi. 8, lxi. 1, 11, lxv. 13, 15. Jeremiah (5 times in vocative), i. 6, iv. 10, xiv. 13, xxxii. (xxxix) 17, 25; (9 times in other cases), ii. 22, vii. 20, xliv. (li) 26, and (with addition of צבאות) ii. 19, xlvi. (xxvi) 10 a, b, xlix (xxx) 5, l. (xxvii) 25, 31. The figures (in brackets) give the chapters as found in the LXX. Amos (21 times, 2 in voc., 19 in other cases), vii. 2, 5; i. 8, iii. 7, 8, 11, 13, iv. 2, 5, v. 3, vi. 8, vii. 1, 4 a, b, 6, viii. 1, 3, 9, 11, ix. 5, 8. The twelve (5 times), Obad. 1, Mic. i. 2, Zeph. i. 7, Zech. ix. 14, Hab. iii. 19. Ezekiel (217 times, 5 only in voc., viz. iv. 14, ix. 8, xi. 13, xxi. 5, xxxvii. 3); in chapters i–xxxix, 195 not in voc., in xl–xlviii, 17 not in voc.

§ Psalms, 4 times 'ᵉ 'א (in voc.), lxix. 7, lxxi. 5, 16; (not in voc.), lxxiii. 28 and 4 times 'א 'ᵉ (in voc.), cix. 21, cxl. 8, cxli. 8 (not in voc.), lxviii. 21. cf. Hab. iii. 19 (see p. 111).

amalgam of J and E, but also shews distinct evidence of
Deuteronomic editing. The phrases 'I am thy shield', 'I am
Yahweh that brought thee out of Ur of the Chaldees, to give
thee this land to inherit it', 'the Great River' all point to the
Deuteronomist, and the only other passages in the Pentateuch
where the double name is used are in Deuteronomy, viz.
iii. 24, ix. 26. In the Former Prophets, of the 11 occurrences,
10 are in the vocative in address to God, the only exception
being in 1 Kings ii. 26. But in the Later Prophets out of
282 occurrences only 12 are in address to God (5 in Jeremiah,
5 in Ezekiel, 2 in Amos). In the Kᵉthuvim probably half the
occurrences are in the vocative (Psalm lxxi. 16 is doubtful)
and that in Hab. iii. 19 is in the same.

Alongside this use of the double name we must observe the
use of אדני by itself (Table I).

> In the Pentateuch אדני occurs 14 times.*
> In the Former Prophets it occurs 8 times.†
> In the Later Prophets 37 times.‡
> In the Kᵉthuvim 78 times,§ in all 137 times.

---

* Gen. xviii. 3, 27, 30, 31, 32, xix. 18, xx. 4, Exod. iv. 10, 13, v. 22,
xv. 17, xxxiv. 9 a, b, Num. xiv. 17.

† Josh. vii. 8, Judges vi. 15, xiii. 8, 1 Kings iii. 10, 15?, xxii. 6,
2 Kings vii. 6, xix. 23.

‡ Isa. iii. 17, 18, iv. 4, vi. 1, 8, 11, vii. 14, 20, viii. 7, ix. 7, 16,
x. 12, 16, xi. 11, xxi. 6, 8, 16, xxviii. 2, xxix. 13, xxx. 20, xxxvii. 24,
xxxviii. 14 (Baer), 16, xlix. 14, Ezek. xv. 25, 29 (xxi. 14 Baer), xxxiii. 17,
20, Amos v. 16, vii. 7, 8, ix. 1, Micah i. 2, Zech. ix. 4, Mal. i. 12
(Baer), 14.

§ Psalms ii. 4, xvi. 2, xxii. 31, xxxv. 17, 22, 23, xxxvii. 13, xxxviii. 10,
16, 23, xxxix. 8, xl. 18, xliv. 24, li. 17, liv. 6, lv. 10, lvii. 10, lix. 12,
lxii. 13, lxvi. 18, lxviii. 12, 18, 20, 23, 27, 33, lxxiii. 20, 28, lxxvii. 3, 8,
lxxviii. 65, lxxix. 12, lxxxvi. 3, 4, 5, 8, 9, 12, 15, lxxxix. 48 (MT אֲנִי),
50, 51, xc. 1, cx. 5, cxxx. 2, 3, 6, Job xxviii. 28, Lam. i. 14, 15 a, b,
ii. 1, 2, 5, 7, 18, 19, 20, iii. 31, 36, 37, 58, v.l. v. 21, Dan. i. 2, ix. 3, 4, 7,
8, 9, 15, 16, 17, 19 (thrice), Neh. i. 11, iv. 8 (E.V 14). In all 137 times.

The occurrences in the Pentateuch are in 13 cases in address
to God, and, if we follow the LXX (Num. xiv. 17), the four-
teenth will also be in the vocative.*

The three occurrences in Joshua and Judges are all in the
vocative in address to God, but the other five occurrences in
the Former Prophets are none of them in address to God. In
the Later Prophets only three of the 37 are in address to God,
but in the Kᵉthuvim half (39 out of 78) are so addressed.

The same difference between early and late usage is observable with אדני as with א׳ י׳. It is only used in address to
God three times in Isaiah (vi. 11, xxi. 8, xxxviii. 16) and in the
Kᵉthuvim eight times in Daniel, once in Lam. (iii. 58), once in
Nehemiah (i. 11), but as one would expect more often (29 times)
in the Psalms. On the other hand in Isaiah (21 times), Psalms
(17) and Lamentations (13) we find fairly frequent use of אדני
otherwise than in address to God. Others so use it, but very
sparingly, Ezekiel (4 times in the mouth of the people and
once in a dubious text xxi. 14), Amos (4), Micah (1), Zechariah
(1), Malachi (2 or 1) and so in the Kᵉthuvim, Job (1), Daniel
(4), Nehemiah (1 or 2).

Turning now to the LXX, we note that

1. In regard to the אדני standing alone the regular translation throughout is κύριος with or without the article. The
usage of κύριος for אדני is in the main on the same lines as
that of κύριος for יהוה; but in the vocative and in address to
God in the third person singular it is sometimes translated
by κύριέ μου or κύριός μου (occasionally ὁ κύριός μου). In these
cases the LXX took אדני as appellative with possessive genitive.

---

* In MT of Num. xiv. 17 אדני is determined by the preceding
construct form, but the phrase is unique. The LXX reads כֹּחַ and
the אדני is translated as in the vocative. It is followed by 'as thou
hast said', and therefore in all probability this אדני should be in the
vocative.

In Dan. ix δέσποτα is used five times for the vocative, always without the article.

2. In the case of the double Divine name, we find a variety of renderings (see Table II, pp. 150 f.).

In Gen. xv. 2, 8 the LXX has Δέσποτα κύριε in both verses. Unfortunately in verse 2 B and A are both defective, but *D* so reads, and in verse 8 the reading is given by A*DM*.*

In Deut. iii. 24 the first hand of B and the Bohairic renders κύριε ὁ θεός, while all other MSS. and versions have κύριε κύριε; in ix. 26 Ba₂ and the Ethiopic have κύριε βασιλεῦ τῶν θεῶν, while AF GMΘ rel. Boh. and Lat. insert a second κύριε before βασιλεῦ and there are other minor variants. B's phrase in ix. 26 is unique. Can it be either epexegetic of אֲדֹנָי (by inversion) or due to a secondary hand? The reading of the other MSS. seems to combine two renderings.†

In *the Former Prophets* we find a variety of renderings. The double Name is rendered in B in six different ways:‡ four

* xv. 2 Δέσποτα κύριε *D*amnoqux c₂ Arm.; om L: om Δέσποτα a* Sah.: om κύριε Mb–hj(txt)lprs(txt)tvwyd₂ Boh. Eth. Phil. Chr.⅔ Cyr.⅔ Codd.⅓ Jul. ap. Cyr.

xv. 8 Δέσποτα κύριε A*DM* abdeghjl–ye₂ Arm. Boh. Eth. Lat. κύριε θεέ Sah. Phil.-codd.: om Δέσποτα f: om κύριε U₄ Phil.-ed. Cyr.½: + θεέ bw.

† Dt. ix. 26 κύριε Ba₂ Eth. + κε AFGMNΘ rell. Arm.-ed. Boh. Lat.ʳ Phil.: Domine Domine Deus Lat.ᶻ: + Deus Arm.-codd.

βασιλεῦ τῶν θεῶν] sub G: om K.

θεῶν] ἔθνων s(mg)uv(mg)z(mg) a₂ Bohˡᵛ: αἰώνων bw.

‡ κύριέ μου κύριε 5 times, Judges vi. 22, 2 Sam. vii. 18, 19b, 28, 29; in A twice, 2 Sam. vii. 18, 29.

κύριέ μου once, 2 Sam. vii. 19a; in A thrice, 2 Sam. vii. 19a, b, 28.

κύριε κύριε once, 1 Kings viii. 53; in A thrice, Josh. vii. 7, Judges vi. 22, xvi. 28.

ἀδωναιὲ κύριε once, Judges xvi. 28; not in A, see above.

κύριε twice, Josh. vii. 7, 2 Sam. vii. 20; in A once, 2 Sam. vii. 20.

κυρίου once, 1 Kings ii. 26; in A once, 1 Kings ii. 26; missing once 1 Kings viii. 53.

times a single name and seven times a double name in three different forms. A five times has a single name and five times a double name in two forms and once omits a Divine name altogether. Moreover, we note that in B the once read ἀδωναιὲ κύριε occurs in Judges xvi. 28, i.e. in that portion of the MS. which is universally recognized as a translation later in time than the rest. AGM, various cursives and the Armenian, Ethiopic and Syro-Hexaplar here read κύριε κύριε.*

In *the Later Prophets* we have apparent chaos. In *Isaiah* we meet with no examples of the vocative, but there are 25 occurrences of the double Divine name, which are rendered by B in four different ways, viz.:

---

* In the one case which is not in the vocative (1 Kings ii. 26) all the Hebrew MSS. read אֲרוֹן א׳ ׳י, whereas elsewhere the phrase is always אֲרוֹן ׳י (Josh. iii. 13 ff., 17, iv. 7, 9, 11 (16), 18, vi. 8 f. (LXX), viii. 33, etc.) and never אֲרוֹן א׳. Probably the original reading here also was אֲרוֹן ׳י and is correctly rendered by the LXX, so far as the Divine name is concerned, by κυρίου. But the addition in the LXX of τῆς διαθήκης in 1 Kings ii. 26 and a comparison with the LXX of Josh. iii. 13, 17, etc., forbid one's putting too much trust here in the evidence of the LXX.

In Judges xiii. 8 simple אֲדֹנָי is rendered in B κύριε ἀδωναιὲ ejqsza₂ Sah. ἀδωναί: om AMN rell. Arm. Eth. Lat. Syr.

In 2 Sam. vii. 22, BAy Sah. render Κύριε κύριέ μου] (om Eth.: om κύριε av; Κύριέ μου κύριε MN rell. Arm. Orig.-Gr.) for MT אֱלֹהִים ׳י as if ׳י א׳.

In 2 Sam. vii. 25 we have again in MT ׳י אֱלֹהִים, which B renders κύριέ μου and so also Axya₂ Arm.: pr. Deus Sah.: Deus Lʳ: Domine Eth.: + κύριε MN rell. Theodt.

In 1 Sam. i. 11 MT has ׳י צְבָאוֹת. Here B has ᾿Αδωναὶ κύριε ᾿Ελωὲ σαβαώθ and A has ᾿Αδωναὶ καὶ ᾿Ελωὲ σαβαώθ, which may be duplication of versions, but the last three words of B are the equivalent of ׳י אֱלֹהֵי צְבָאוֹת, a secondary expansion which fairly often occurs. The pronunciation of ᾿Αδωναί for ׳י is therefore relatively old.

κύριος κύριος 10 times (in every case A omits one κύριος).
κύριος ὁ θεός once (A omits κύριος). The reading in B gives
the MT pronunciation.
κύριος Σαβαώθ once.
κύριος alone 11 times.
The Divine name is wanting in two passages.

The position is complicated in the first thirty-nine chapters
by the addition to the double name in eight passages of צְבָאוֹת
and in four passages (not included in the 25) by the phrase
הָאָדוֹן יְ צְבָאוֹת, which is once translated κύριος ὁ δεσπότης Σαβαώθ,
once ὁ δεσπότης κύριος Σαβαώθ, and twice κύριος Σαβαώθ. In
vii. 7 the יְ אֲ is rendered κύριος Σαβαώθ.*

---

* κύριος κύριος xxii. 12, xxviii. 16, xxx. 15; xl. 10, xlviii. 16, l. 4, 5,
7, lii. 4, lxi. 11.
κύριος ὁ θεός xxv. 8 (om κύριος AQΓ), cf. x. 23.
κύριος Σαβαώθ vii. 7.
κύριος x. 23, 24, xxii. 5, 15, xxviii. 22; xlix. 22, l. 9, lvi. 8, lxi. 1,
lxv. 13, 15.
Name omitted iii. 15, xxii. 14 (א^{c,a} + κύριος + (θ^1 σ^1) κύριος κύριος
τῶν δυνάμεων Q^{mg}). Instead of κύριος κύριος we find simple κύριος
10 times in xxii. 12 AQ*Γ, xxviii. 16 אAQ*Γ, xxx. 15 אA, xl. 10
א*AQΓ, xlviii. 16 אAQ*, l. 4 אAQ*, 5 א*AQ*, 7 א^{c,b}AQ*, lii. 4
אAQ*Γ, lxi. 11 אAQ*. Instead of simple κύριος or omission we find
κύριος κύριος iii. 15 Q^{mg}*, x. 24 א^{c,c} (but κύριος ὁ θεός א*AΓ, κύριος
א$^{c,b[vid]}$, xxii. 15 Q^{mg}, xlix. 22 B^a, ^{b}Q^{mg}, l. 9 B^{a,b}Q^{mg}, lvi. 8 Q^{mg},
lxi. 1 *Q^{mg}.
In the following passages in MT צְבָאוֹת is added to the double
name: iii. 15 (B omits, Q^{mg} + * φησὶ κύριος κύριος [πιπι πιπι]
στρατείων + σ^1 λέγει κύριος τῶν δυνάμεων) x. 23, 24, xxii. 5, 12, 14,
15, xxviii. 22 where B has Σαβαώθ in the verses italicized. In four
passages the phrase הָאָדוֹן יְ צְבָאוֹת is translated in B (i. 24) κύριος ὁ
δεσπότης Σαβαώθ (אAQΓ ὁ δεσπότης κύριος Σαβαώθ), iii. 1, x. 33
ὁ δεσπότης κύριος Σαβαώθ, xix. 4 κύριος Σαβαώθ and cf. x. 16. In vii.
7 the double name is rendered κύριος Σαβαώθ though there is no
צְבָאוֹת in MT.

We may sum up the usage in Isaiah by saying that in chapters i–xxxix we have

in B 7 κύριος (incl. vii. 7) and in A 9 (incl. xxviii. 16, xxx. 15),

    3 κύριος κύριος   ,,   none,

    1 κύριος ὁ θεός   ,,   2 ὁ θεός alone (x. 23, xxv. 8),

    1 lacking   ,,   1 lacking,

and in chapters xl–lxvi

in B 5 κύριος   and in A 13 κύριος,

    8 κύριος κύριος.

In Isaiah therefore A stands consistently for the single Divine name and B in 12 passages for the double name, thus reversing the usual relation between the two. It would seem that A in Isaiah had an early MS. as exemplar.

In *Jeremiah*, out of 14 occurrences of the double name five are in the vocative and nine in other cases.*

In *Amos* we find 21 occurrences of the double name in MT, two of which are in the vocative.†

---

* In four of the vocatives, MT has אֲדֹנָי א' יְהוִה. In three of these the LXX reads the first word as אֶהְיֶה (as in Exod. iii. 14) and renders ὁ ὤν (i. 6, xiv. 13, xxxii. 17, in the fourth it translates simply Ὦ (iv. 10). In the fifth case (xxxii. 25) BA, etc. give no rendering. Q^mg adds ✷ κύριε. The double name is rendered by BA twice δέσποτα κύριε (i. 6, iv. 10 and by A also xiv. 13), by B twice κύριε alone (xiv. 13, xxxii. 17), by AQ once κύριε κύριε (xxxii. 17). The nine occurrences not in vocative are rendered in B κύριος five times (ii. 22, vii. 20, xliv. 26, xlix. 5, l. 31), τῷ κυρίῳ once (xlvi. 10b) and once each κύριος ὁ θεός σου (ii. 19), κυρίῳ τῷ θεῷ ἡμῶν (xlvi. 10a) and τῷ κυρίῳ θεῷ (l. 25). In five cases צְבָאוֹת is added in MT (ii. 19, xlvi. 10a, xlix. 5, l. 25, 31, but this is not supported by B and by AQ only in xlvi. 10b. A in ii. 22 has κύριος ὁ θεός σου and אAQ has κύριος κύριος in xliv. 26.

† The two vocatives are translated once κύριε κύριε (vii. 2), once κύριε B, but + κύριε AQ (vii. 5). The other 19 are represented in B by κύριος seven times (i. 8, iv. 2, vi. 8, vii. 4 a, b, 6, viii. 11), in AQ also vii. 1 and in Q* viii. 3. κύριος κύριος four times (v. 3,

In *the rest of the Minor Prophets* the double name occurs five times. In four B witnesses to a double name, though by varied renderings; by κύριος κύριος Mic. i. 2 (but AQ omit 2nd κύριος and Q^mg has κύριος ὁ θεός), κύριος ὁ θεός Obad. 1, κυρίου τοῦ θεοῦ Zeph. i. 7, κύριος παντοκράτωρ Zech. ix. 14 (cf. 15 κύριος παντοκράτωρ = צְבָאוֹת.."). Moreover in Mic. vi. 1 simple ײ is translated κύριος κύριος and in Jonah iv. 3 δέσποτα κύριε (Table II, pp. 150 f.). The fifth is Hab. iii. 19. (See below.)

Baudissin urges that there is clear witness in the Prophets to the genuineness of the double name in the vocative by the renderings κύριε κύριε and δέσποτα κύριε, but that in the other cases the variety of renderings and the frequent use of κύριος alone do not give clear witness.

In *the K^ethuvim* the occurrences of the double name are but eight, including four in inverted order, and are confined to the Book of Psalms; cf. Hab. iii, which is itself a Psalm. The earlier Psalms translate by κύριε alone (lxix. 7, lxxi. 5, 16 in the vocative) and in lxxiii. 28 by ἐν τῷ κυρίῳ (though lxxi. 5 κύριος, κύριος might be taken as dividing the ײ א between the two halves of the verse). The inverted double name occurs in lxviii (lxvii) 21 B τοῦ κυρίου (א^ca R^a + κυρίου) and in cix. 21, cxl. 8, cxli. 8; cf. Hab. iii. 19, where it is three times translated by κύριε κύριε and in Habakkuk by κύριος ὁ θεός. It would seem as though here the inversion and the double name itself were authentic in the later period,

viii. 1, 3, 9); also κύριε κύριε vii. 5 AQ; κύριος κύριος vii. 6 Q, viii. 3, 11 Qa. κύριος ὁ θεός seven times (iii. 7, 8, 11, 13, iv. 5, vii. 1, ix. 8); also A vii. 4a, AQ viii. 9, Q^mg vii. 4b; pr. κύριος Q^a; ὁ θεός v. 3 Q^a. In three cases MT adds אֱלֹהֵי הַצְּבָאוֹת or הַצְּבָאוֹת alone and twice B has κύριος ὁ θεός ὁ παντοκράτωρ (iii. 13, v. 16), once κύριος κύριος ὁ παντοκράτωρ (ix. 5). In v. 16 the order is יהוה אלהי צבאות אדני. In v. 15 κύριος ὁ θεός ὁ παντοκράτωρ is for י' אלהי'צבאות. In three passages אדני occurs by itself and is translated by LXX κύριος (vii. 7, 8), or τὸν κύριον (ix. 1).

when the last two books of the Psalms were written and collected.

II. We now come face to face with the supreme element in the problem of the Divine names in the Old Testament, viz. that which presents itself in the Book of Ezekiel.

We noted at the outset of our study that out of 305 occurrences of the double name in the Old Testament 217 are found in Ezekiel and that, whereas in the MT the usage in that Book is regular and uniform, in the LXX, as represented by B, the corresponding usage is extremely irregular, אדני יהוה being represented in B* by simple κύριος 139 times, by κύριος κύριος 54 times, by ἀδωναὶ κύριος twice and (in xl–xlviii) by κύριος ὁ θεός seven times and by κύριος θεός nine times, + four omissions. How can we explain these phenomena? (see Table IV, pp. 153 ff.).

(i) We must note in the first place the remarkable divergences of the MSS. in the LXX in Ezekiel.*

Take first the chapters i to xxxix. The only five vocatives are found in this part of the Book. They are translated in three different ways in B (four in A and Q):

κύριε ix. 8 (ἀδωναὶ κύριε AQ).
κύριε xi. 13 (ἀδωναὶ κύριε AQ).
κύριε xxxvii. 3 (κύριε κύριε AQ).

---

* B (Codex Vaticanus) is generally regarded as representing best the original text of the LXX and is attributed to the fourth century.

A (Codex Alexandrinus) is probably a century later in date.

Q (Codex Marchalliensis) was written in Egypt not later than the sixth century. Its text is regarded by Ceriani as Hesychian, but hexaplaric signs have been freely added and in the margin copious extracts from Aquila, Symmachus and Theodotion and the LXX of the Hexapla have been added in a hand not much later than that of the original MS. Table V shews at a glance the diversity of witness of these MSS (p. 160).

א (Codex Sinaiticus) is unfortunately lacking.

κύριε κύριε xxi. 5 (κύριε κύριε AQ).

κύριε θεὲ τοῦ 'Ισραήλ iv. 14 (κύριε κύριε θεὲ τοῦ 'Ισραήλ A; κύριε ὁ θεὸς τοῦ 'Ισραήλ Q).

Taking now the whole 200 occurrences in these thirty-nine chapters, we find

	In B	In A	In Q
κύριος	139	37	2
κύριος κύριος	54	63	99
ἀδωναὶ κύριος	2	82	97
Omissions	4	–	1
κύριος (ὁ) θεός	–	17	1
κύριε θεὲ τοῦ 'Ισραήλ	1	1	–
	200	200	200

Is it possible that, as Baudissin would have us believe, the original LXX everywhere read simple κύριος?

(ii) We will consider first the 54 κύριος κύριος in B. Broadly speaking we may say that up to xx. 38 B almost invariably has κύριος, up to chapter xxx it uses κύριος κύριος only sporadically, from chapters xxx to xxxix it uses κύριος κύριος in the large majority of cases* (see Table VI, pp. 161 f.).

Κύριος κύριος seems clearly to witness to the double name אד' י'.

It is a question whether the original pronunciation would be Adonai Yahweh or Adonai Adonai. Von Baudissin thinks that the Synagogue hearer, when he heard אדני pronounced for יהוה, thought not of the literal meaning, but of the Sacred name which it represented (just as when he heard בּשֶׁת pronounced for בַּעַל [ἡ αἰσχύνη for ὁ βάαλ] he thought of the idol, not of the literal meaning) and that the double name would

---

* In the 54 cases, where B has κύριος κύριος, A has in three cases simple κύριος (xxviii. 12, xxxv. 3, xxxvi. 5), but in the other 51 it reads 20 times κύριος κύριος, 14 times κύριος κύριος ὁ θεός, 4 κύριος ὁ θεός, 10 ἀδωναὶ κύριος, 1 ἀδωναὶ κύριος κύριος, 2 ἀδωναὶ κύριος ὁ θεός. In the same 54 passages Q has 52 κύριος κύριος, 2 ἀδωναὶ κύριος.

be pronounced אֲדֹנִי אֲדֹנִי, it being understood at once that
the second pronounced אֲדֹנִי represented יהוה. This would be
obvious and intelligible to the Jewish hearers, though now
it seems abstruse to us. To the eye of the Reader א' י' were
different words, but he pronounced them identically and his
hearers understood. At a later time, to avoid the identical
double pronunciation, the pronunciation handed down by the
Masora came in, by which for the Sacred name the general
name אלהים was substituted in the general public reading.

(iii) Before carrying further the discussion on the force of
κύριος κύριος, we will now consider the alternative rendering
ἀδωναὶ κύριος. This reading only occurs twice in B, viz. in
xxxvi. 33, 37 (B^{ab} reads the same in xxxvi. 32, where B*Q
have κύριος κύριος and A has κύριος ὁ θεός). As Thackeray
pointed out in the *Journal of Theological Studies* for April 1903,
'the Greek of Ezekiel xxxvi. 24–38 (the section on "the new
heart") markedly stands out from that of the rest of this part
of the book'. This section seems to have been read at a very
early time as a Pentecostal lesson in the Jewish Synagogue,
just as in our Prayer-Book Calendar this passage is an alternative lesson for the evening of Whitsunday. And it may be
reasonably conjectured that an early translation of the lesson
was incorporated into the LXX.

But while B only reads ἀδωναὶ κύριος twice (or thrice) in the
first thirty-nine chapters A reads it 82 times (where B has
κύριος 70 times, κύριος κύριος 10 times and 2 are lacking) and
Q reads it 97 times (B 94 κύριος, 2 κύριος κύριος [xxviii. 25,
xxxiv. 18] and 1 is lacking). Moreover in A ἀδωναὶ κύριος is
found in combination with other readings, viz. ἀδωναὶ κύριος
κύριος twice (xxvi. 15, xxvii. 3), ἀδωναὶ κύριος κύριος ὁ θεός
(xxiii. 32) once. 'Αδωναὶ κύριος in A and Q stands almost exclusively where the double name occurs in MT and clearly
witnesses to its being in the Hebrew text when A and Q were

copied. Baudissin urges that it must have come in, not only after the original translation (witnessed to by B) was made, but also some time after κύριος κύριος came into use, and that it was inserted mainly in passages where that rendering was not already in possession.

(iv) It is noteworthy that in the codices of the LXX which are reckoned to belong to the Lucianic (Antiochene) recension,* ἀδωναί κύριος occurs in 25 out of the 54 places where B has κύριος κύριος. Six of these occur in the same places where ἀδωναί κύριος occurs in A, but 19 do not.

How did this rendering come about? One answer to this question is given by Jacob of Edessa in a Scholium to his translation (made in A.D. 701) of the Λόγοι ἐπιθρόνιοι of the Patriarch Severus of Antioch. In this Scholium he says that the LXX originally did not translate the tetragrammaton but reproduced it in its Hebrew characters, but that 'the others' wrote ἀδωναί in the text and κύριος in the margin. 'Lucian', he goes on to say, 'as he read ἀδωναί in the text and κύριος in the margin combined the two and set them down together. This he did in such cases as "Thus spake ἀδωναί κύριος" and "the spirit of 'Αδωναί κύριος fell upon me" and 'Αδωναί κύριος did or said this or that.' This statement is only partially true of the codices we regard as Lucianic. Von Baudissin thinks there must be a substratum of fact, but questions the assertion that ἀδωναί was put in the text and κύριος in the margin and suggests that the opposite was the actual fact. It is a question whether Jacob of Edessa had ever himself seen the MSS. from which he says that Lucian had derived his ἀδωναί κύριος. He seems

* The LXX MSS. usually regarded as Lucianic and which contain (parts of) Ezekiel are 22, 36, 42, 48, 51, 62, 90, 153, 233. (See Field's Prolegg. p. lxxxiv f. and Lagarde, Prolegomena to *Librorum V.T. Canon. Pars prior Graece*, p. 14, Swete's Introd. pp. 82 f., 165 ff.)

to refer to 'the others' as translators, but his statement does not agree with the usage of the only other translators known to us, viz. Aquila, Symmachus and Theodotion, and in reality he probably refers to a group of LXX MSS. His statement that the LXX reproduced the Sacred name in Hebrew characters does fit in with the usage of Aquila and perhaps Symmachus, and he may have regarded these as the original LXX. His explanation of the placing of κύριος in the margin as being due to a timidity which prevented them from translating the Sacred name can hardly be right, for the procedure seems to have been confined practically to the two combinations with כֹּה אָמַר and נְאֻם and, if his statement were correct, the procedure would have been carried out wherever יהוה occurs, whereas the Lucianic MSS. practically only use ἀδωναὶ κύριος where in MT the double name occurs. Forty-four out of the total 46 occurrences in these MSS. do concur with the double name in MT and 39 of these are in combinations with τάδε λέγει or λέγει. Only in two places does 'Αδωναὶ κύριος stand in these MSS. for a simple י in MT. Clearly the writer cannot have been afraid of translating the word י per se. The copyists must have known the reading א׳ י׳ either in their exemplars or otherwise.

It cannot be accidental that, in the 54 places where B has κύριος κύριος for א׳ י׳, the Lucianic MSS., as we have seen, have 25 ἀδωναὶ κύριος, i.e. nearly half the total, whereas in the 146 places where B has not got κύριος κύριος the Lucianic MSS. have ἀδωναὶ κύριος in only 19, i.e. only one in eight, and in these places often only in a single MS. Clearly the ἀδωναὶ κύριος of the Lucianic MSS., the κύριος κύριος of B and the א׳ י׳ of the MT in general correspond with one another. The two former clearly go back to an exemplar which contained the double Divine name. On the other hand we note that while in six cases A and the Lucianic MSS. agree in reading ἀδωναὶ κύριος for the κύριος κύριος in B and in 14 cases A (10) or Q (13) and the Lucianic MSS. agree in reading ἀδωναὶ κύριος where B has simple κύριος for ʼ ʼא, yet in a very much larger number of cases A (70) and Q (94) have this reading for the simple κύριος in B, where the Lucianic MSS. have not got it.*

If B is the nearer to the original, ἀδωναί is an insertion by a later hand in order to accommodate the LXX to the revised MT. As already noted (p. 113, note *) A has simple κύριος in three places where B has κύριος κύριος. If possibly A preserves the original reading in these three cases, may not the same reading have originally stood where κύριος κύριος now stands in B?

While in the 54 places where B has κύριος κύριος either A or Q or most often both also have κύριος κύριος, in the 139 passages in which MT has the double name and B has the simple κύριος, A 70 times and Q 94 times have ἀδωναὶ κύριος. It would

* A has ἀδωναὶ κύριος 49 times in i–xx (48 with Q, once without xii. 28) where B everywhere has κύριος only and 33 times in xxi–xxxix (13 with Q where B has κύριος + xxxiii. 11 in Aᵃ, once with Q sub * where B has κύριος xxxvi. 23 and 8 times without Q where B has κύριος and 10 times without Q where B has κύριος κύριος (Q in all these cases is = B) and once where B and Q have nothing xxxiii. 25. (Aᵃ has ἀδωναὶ κύριος 10 or 11 times more.)

Q* has ἀδωναὶ κύριος 66 times in i–xx (48 with A and 18 alone) and 31 times in xxi–xxxix (14 with A, 14 without A, B having κύριος 27 out of the 28 times, twice without A where B has κύριος κύριος xxviii. 25, xxxiv. 8 and once without either B or A sub * xxxvi. 7).

Of these cases B has simple κύριος against AQ 62 times, against A alone 19 times, against Q alone 35 times; and κύριος κύριος 10 times against A and twice against Q.

A, and Q (with two exceptions) read ἀδωναὶ κύριος only where MT has ʼ ʼא. The two possible exceptions are xxi. 14 (9) in AᵃQ where probably MT originally had ʼ ʼא and xxiv. 20 where MT has ʼ alone and A¹ has τάδε λέγει ἀδωναὶ κύριος sup ras, but Q omits any Divine name.

appear from this that in A and Q ἀδωναί has been inserted
deliberately in the passages where the Hebrew double name
has not already been expressed by κύριος κύριος. There still
remain in A 34 cases where simple κύριος is used for the
double name and three cases where B gives no Divine name.
In Q in like case simple κύριος is only twice found (xii. 28 b,
xxiv. 49). If ἀδωναί has been inserted in front of κύριος by a
later hand (in A 69 times, in Q 32), then in the 139 cases of
simple κύριος in B 100 are supported, when ἀδωναί is eliminated,
by either one or both of the two MSS., A and Q. In the
passages outside Ezekiel, in which in MT the double Divine
name is now found, neither in the Lucianic MSS. nor in other
MSS. including A and Q does ἀδωναί κύριος occur, with two
exceptions: viz. the vocative ἀδωναί κύριος B in Judges xvi. 28,
where in all probability it does not belong to the early LXX
text* and ἀδωναί κύριε B (A) Luc. for יהוה in 1 Sam. i. 11 MT,
which may represent an original א׳ י׳. If this be read, we
note that it is in the vocative as in the other passage.

(v) The Old Latin version, where extant,† with two doubtful
exceptions, in the places where the MT has the double name,
everywhere has 'dominus'. As the Old Latin was at least in
the main a translation from the LXX, we may reasonably
conclude that their exemplar had κύριος alone. It has 'dominus'
in 19 places where B has κύριος κύριος and it thus raises doubt
as to the originality of the B text in these places. None of

* The κύριε ἀδωναιέ B of Judges xiii. 8 for אֲדֹנָי alone falls into the
same category and is also in the vocative.

† We have MSS of the Itala extant containing chapters viii and
xvi–xxxviii, but with many gaps. The Codex Weingartensis in 31
places has simple 'dominus' for א׳ י׳. Codex Wirceburgensis has
16 places, of which three are the same as C. Weingartensis. The
'dominus' in these two MSS. corresponds in 19 places with a κύριος
κύριος in B. Only in xxxii. 31 does C. Weingartensis seem to read
'Dominus Deus'.

these 19 times are in the vocative. In like manner Tyconius
in his citations from Ezekiel (taken from chapters xx to xxxvii
only) with one exception has everywhere 'dominus' for ʼא ʼי.
The one exception (xxxvi. 33) agrees with B in witnessing
there to the double name. This is to be explained, as on p. 114,
as coming from a Pentecostal lesson independently translated
and adopted into the LXX.

Since in xl–xlviii the Old Latin generally reads 'Dominus
Deus' for the κύριος (ὁ) θεός of these chapters, never a
simple 'Dominus', it would seem natural to conclude that
its LXX exemplar in i–xxxix had a simple κύριος corresponding to the simple 'dominus' there witnessed to. In the
one doubtful case (xxxii. 31) it is possible that the MS.
(probably originally of the third century) has been altered
under the influence of the Vulgate, but it is more probable
that the 'Dominus Deus' of xl–xlviii has in this one place
been imported from thence into i–xxxix at a later date. The
Sangalliensis MS. in xl–xlviii has once (xlviii. 29) 'Dominus
Deus' (agreeing with Weingartensis); in i–xxxix it has single
'Dominus' 81 times for ʼא ʼי (in 20 cases it agrees with
Weingartensis and Wirceburgensis, in the other 61 passages
the other MSS. are not extant), and only twice has 'Dominus
Deus' (xxiii. 24, xxxiv. 17). The two exceptions seem to
be explicable on the same lines as that of xxxii. 31 in Codex
Weingartensis above.

(vi) All translations which are not made from the LXX
express the double Divine name. The Targum has for ʼא ʼי
everywhere יהוה אלהים in accordance with MT pronunciation.
The Peshito with two exceptions (xxiii. 49, xxxix. 13) and the
Vulgate agree with this. They had ʼא ʼי clearly in the text
which they had before them, but their date makes it impossible
to arrive at definite conclusions as to the original LXX
text.

(vii) The rendering κύριος ὁ θεός in one form or another*
occurs 17 times in A and once in Q (xx. 5) in chapters i–xxxix.
We will deal with this rendering in the next section.

Chapters xl–xlviii. So far we have been examining the
usage of the LXX in i–xxxix. On turning to xl–xlviii we find
a very different state of things—a difference which only seems
explicable, if we fully recognize the special and independent
position of these chapters. י 'א occurs 17 times in the MT of
these chapters, the first occurrence being in xliii. In B it is
represented six times by κύριος ὁ θεός (in xliii–xliv), once by
κύριος ὁ θεὸς 'Ισραήλ (xliii. 18), nine times by κύριος θεός
(xlv–xlviii) and once by κύριος alone (xliii. 27). The change
from κύριος ὁ θεός to κύριος θεός is probably due to a change
of copyist. Taking these two forms as practically the same, we
see that B in 16 out of the 17 occurrences witnesses in these
chapters to the double name and renders it by κύριος (ὁ) θεός. A
and Q agree in translating by κύριος ὁ θεός in 11 cases, A alone
in four more and Q alone once (always with the article before
θεός). Alongside these Q five times translates by κύριος κύριος
(xliii. 18, 19, 27, xliv. 6, xlv. 9a), and A once translates by
κύριος (xliii. 27) and once by ἀδωναὶ κύριος. The Old Latin,
where it is extant, with two exceptions confirms the rendering
κύριος (ὁ) θεός by its 'Dominus Deus'. In the one place where
B and A (supported by the Old Latin 'Dominus') have κύριος,
Q witnesses to the double name by its κύριος κύριος. In all probability κύριος ὁ θεός here, as in other of the later prophets,†

---

* κύριος ὁ θεός 12 times, ἀδωναὶ κύριος ὁ θεός twice (xxxvii. 21,
xxxviii. 17) and once each κύριος ὁ θεὸς 'Ισραήλ (xxi. 3 = xx. 47),
ἀδωναὶ κύριος κύριος ὁ θεός (xxiii. 32) and κύριος ὁ θεὸς αὐτῶν (xxviii.
24). κύριος κύριος ὁ θεός occurs 25 times.

† Cf. the seven κύριος ὁ θεός in B in Amos, the one (doubtful)
example in Isaiah and the three in Jeremiah (in three forms) for
 י 'א (pp. 110 note †, 109 note *, 110 note *).

is a rendering of the Qri of MT, i.e. the pronunciation
אֲדֹנָי אֱלֹהִים.*

In all probability not only the 17 κύριος (ὁ) θεός in xl–xlviii
but also the 17 κύριος ὁ θεός and the 25 κύριος κύριος ὁ θεός
of A in i–xxxix all arose from the MT Qri of 'י 'א, even as
we find in Targum, Peshito and Vulgate at a later time. This
probability is further supported by the fact that the Lucianic
MSS. for the 17 'י 'א in xl–xlviii have 11 times ἀδωναὶ κύριος,
which with them in i–xxxix only stands where 'י 'א stands
in MT. In the other six cases they read four times κύριος θεός,
once κύριος ὁ θεός and once (with BA) a simple κύριος (xliii. 27).
The regular use of κύριος (ὁ) θεός in xl–xlviii, if we may judge
from the Old Latin 'Dominus Deus', must be pre-Hexaplaric
and must mean that the Masoretic pronunciation was known
to the translator. The different translation of the double name
in i–xxxix and xl–xlviii may be due to a different translator,
or it may be due to the different usage of a later Hebrew writer
or Editor or to a later pronunciation of the same consonantal
text.

3. Here we must consider another important factor in the
Ezekielian problem, which we have so far left on one side.

---

* Cornill sees in κύριος ὁ θεός a translation of יהוה אלהים as in
Gen. ii. 11, etc. and regards this as having a theological significance,
Ezekiel setting his vision of the New Jerusalem alongside that of
Paradise. But this is very improbable. In other 'Later Prophets'
κύριος ὁ θεός seems to be the translation of the MT Qri of 'י 'א and
so it seems to be here in Ezek. xliii–xlviii. יהוה אלהים with no pronominal suffix or genitive following never occurs in Ezekiel in MT.
In one passage (xliv. 2) יהוה אלהי ישראל occurs, where B and A have
a corresponding κύριος ὁ θεὸς 'Ισραήλ (cf. xliii. 18 B where a copyist
may have added 'Ισραήλ) and in the immediately preceding section
(xxxix. 22, 28); יהוה אלהיהם twice occurs, but in Ezekiel the combination is not frequent (only xx. 5, 7, 19, 20 and xxviii. 26, xxxiv. 30
both in MT and in LXX).

Mr St John Thackeray in the *Journal of Theological Studies* for April 1903 and later in his Schweich Lectures (1920) set forth evidence to shew that an examination of the vocabulary and grammatical usages in the LXX of Ezekiel proved that the Book had been divided into two more or less equal parts and had been translated by different hands. Thackeray regarded the break as occurring between xxvii and xxviii, pointing out, e.g. that צוֹר (Tyre) was translated in xxvi–xxvii by Σόρ, but in xxviii–xxix by Τύρος. He gave further evidence, which seemed to shew that while i–xxvii and xxviii–xxxix were clearly by separate hands, in xl–xlviii the characteristics of the first translator reappeared. Herrmann and Baumgärtel would however regard the translator of xl–xlviii as a third hand.*

Baudissin, on the ground of the changes in translation of the Divine names, was inclined at first to attribute the translation of xxi–xxxix to the second hand, but afterwards was content to leave the question open as to the exact division, seeing that the decision does not at all vitally affect the result as to the change in the treatment of the Divine names. Thackeray himself points out that in xxv and xxvii the two styles seem in certain particulars to stand side by side. And Herrmann recognizes the same tangling between xxi and xxvii.

If now we accept the view that i–xxxix is to be divided into two parts, translated by different hands, we note that in B the variations of rendering fall almost entirely in the second part. Looking at the variations in Table IV between Parts 1 and 2, it is tempting to explain them by saying that the two translators had before them the present Hebrew text, but one

* *Beiträge zur Wissenschaft vom Alten Testament*, N.F. 5, 1923, pp. 1–19 and App. pp. 81–95.

preferred to render by simple κύριος, while the other made large use of κύριος κύριος and, we may add, a third (in xl–xlviii) preferred κύριος ὁ θεός. Herrmann, impressed by the regularity of the usage in the Hebrew and by the patent irregularities in the Greek and by the fact that the large use of κύριος κύριος is practically confined to the second part, believed that we could thus explain the facts.*

Baudissin cannot accept this on the grounds that

(i) The Greek translators nowhere in the whole Old Testament shew any such tendency to abbreviate other Divine names as Herrmann attributes to the first hand.

(ii) The same apparent abbreviating does occur in the translations of other prophets where MT has יי אֲדֹנָי. But it is not probable that these translators would all have made the same wilful shortening in this Divine name alone.

(iii) While in xx. 39 to xxxix. 29, where there are 125 occurrences of יי אֲדֹנָי, κύριος κύριος occurs 49 times in B*, side by side with this, there still stand 69 simple κύριος.

(iv) The Old Latin has 'Dominus' not only in i–xx, but (with one doubtful exception) equally in xxi–xxxix, while in xl–xlviii (with two possible exceptions) it translates by 'Dominus Deus'. Unfortunately, owing to the fragmentary character of our MSS. of the Old Latin, we cannot speak with absolute certainty as to its total usage. The LXX and Old Latin usage then makes us pause before we agree to Herrmann's solution that the MT gives us the author's original text and that the variations of the LXX are due to translators and copyists.

There is common agreement as to the purpose which underlay the use of the double name. Where Jehovah is described as speaking, אֲדֹנָי is added to יי in order to give additional

* In B only 3 κύριος κύριος occur in i to xx. 36 (xii. 10, xiii. 20, xiv. 6), 15 in xx. 39 to xxix. 16, and 36 in xxix. 19 to xxxix. 29.

solemnity, 'א being here used in the sense of a proper name
(= the All Lord). Of the double name י emphasizes the Being
of God and 'א His Lordship. As to the five cases whose
י 'א is used in the vocative, it is most likely that the vocatival
use was a fixed form of address to the Godhead for a long time
before Ezekiel (see pp. 104 f., 111) and it is simplest to give the
pronominal suffix its full value: 'My Lord Jehovah', whereas
in the other uses it is clearly 'the Lord Jehovah'. The meaning
'My Lord Jehovah' would be quite impossible in the formula
put into the mouth of Jehovah 'that I am (my) Lord Jehovah'.
Where on the other hand the phrase is 'the word of Jehovah',
Jehovah Himself is not thought of as the speaker, but Jehovah
is used adjectivally after the Hebrew manner and the word
spoken by the prophet is described as Divine, i.e. as coming
forth from Jehovah. It is very questionable whether the same
author would use 'א sometimes as = 'my Lord' and sometimes as = 'the Lord'. If he would not, then the latter sense
is probably the later use and used by an Editor. The phrase
כִּי אֲנִי יי ('that I am Jehovah'), if not known to Ezekiel, would
be known to a later Editor, as the established usage in Lev.
xvii–xxvi.

The same contrast between the usages in the LXX (B),
which we found when treating of the whole number of uses
of the double name, is also found when we isolate the uses
found in connection with the two phrases כֹּה אָמַר יי and נְאֻם. The
use of י 'א in connection with the first is found 117 times in
i–xxxix. Of these 37 fall in i–xx. 26 and B only 3 times has
κύριος κύριος, whereas 80 fall in xx–xxxix and B 30 times has
κύριος κύριος. The proportion for κύριος κύριος in the two parts
is therefore 3 out of 37 and 30 out of 80, i.e. in the one part
1 out of 13 and in the other 1 out of 2⅔.

A similar situation is found when we turn to the second

phrase. In i–xx. 36 out of 32 uses with נְאֻם B once has κύριος
κύριος. In xx. 39–xxxix. 29 out of 37 uses B has 19 κύριος κύριος.
The proportion for κύριος κύριος in the first part is 1 out of 32,
in the second it is 19 out of 37, i.e. in Part 1, 1 to 32 and in
Part 2, 1 to 2. This points to the same conclusion as before,
viz. that (apart from the vocatives) the original LXX translators, certainly in Part 1 and very possibly in Part 2, did not
find the double name in their Hebrew text and therefore did
not translate it.

Passing to xl–xlviii אֲדֹנָי י only occurs in the above-mentioned
two combinations (8 and 9 times respectively). B (with one
exception, see p. 120) has everywhere κύριος (ὁ) θεός. A (with
the same exception) and Q (without exception) regularly
witness to a double name (A, 15 κύριος ὁ θεός, 1 ἀδωναί κύριος;
Q, 12 κύριος ὁ θεός, 5 κύριος κύριος). The Old Latin, where
extant, exhibits the same phenomenon. These translations exhibit
the Masoretic pronunciation and seem to point to the later date
of the translation of these chapters. Even if Thackeray is right
in holding that the same hand translated i–xxvii and xl–xlviii
(and this is questionable), the last nine chapters may have had
originally a separate existence and have been independently
revised before the translation of the whole Book was made.
Herrmann however, as we have seen (p. 122), gives cogent
reasons for regarding xl–xlviii as having been translated by a
third hand.

It is noteworthy that the MT of Ezekiel stands practically
alone in its well-nigh exclusive use of the double name in
these two formulae (כה אמר and נאם). The double name is
used 56 times in Amos, Isaiah, Jeremiah and Obadiah, but
only 23 times is it used with the two formulae (Amos 7 times
out of 21, Isaiah 10 times out of 25, Jeremiah 5 times out of 9,
Obadiah once).

Amos uses כה אמר twice with א׳ י׳, 12 times with simple י׳,

נאם	5 times	,,	,,	16	,,	,,	,,
אמר	twice	,,	,,	6	,,	,,	,,
Other phrases	12 times	,,	,,	26	,,	,,	,,
making a total of	21 times	,,	,,	60	,,	,,	,, *

For the LXX use, see the footnote below and the next page.

*

MT	AMOS	LXX
2 י׳ א׳ with כה אמר	iii. 11	BAQ κύριος ὁ θεός (om ὁ Ab)
(to 12 simple י׳)	v. 3	BAQ* κύριος κύριος (Qa κύριος ὁ θεός)
5 י׳ א׳ with נאם	iii. 13	BAQ κύριος ὁ θεός (ὁ παντοκράτωρ
(to 16 with simple י׳)		= Heb. אֱלֹהֵי הַצְּבָאוֹת)
	iv. 5	BAQ κύριος ὁ θεός
	viii. 3	BAQa κύριος κύριος, Q* κύριος
	viii. 9	B κύριος κύριος, AQ κύριος ὁ θεός
	viii. 11	BA κύριος, Qa κύριος κύριος
2 י׳ א׳ with אמר	i. 8	BAQ κύριος
(to 6 with simple י׳)	vii. 6	BA κύριος, Q κύριος κύριος
12 י׳ א׳ with neither	iii. 7	BAQ κύριος ὁ θεός
formula	iii. 8	BAQ κύριος ὁ θεός
(to 26 with simple י׳)	iv. 2	BAQ κύριος
	vi. 8	BAQ κύριος
	vii. 1	B κύριος ὁ θεός, AQ om ὁ θεός, Qa κύριος κύριος
(vocative)	vii. 2	BAQ κύριε κύριε
	vii. 4 a	B κύριος, A κύριος ὁ θεός, Qa κύριος κύριος
	vii. 4 b	BA κύριος, Qmg κύριος ὁ θεός
(vocative)	vii. 5	B κύριε, AQ κύριε κύριε
	viii. 1	BAQ κύριος κύριος
(+ הצבאות)	ix. 5	κύριος κύριος ὁ θεὸς ὁ παντοκράτωρ
	ix. 8	κυρίου τοῦ θεοῦ
Note also the following:	vii. 3, 6 a, 8 a	4 times י׳ alone, BAQ κύριος and κύριε
	vii. 4 c	not in MT, B κυρίου, AQ = MT
	vii. 7 a, 8 b	twice א׳ alone, BAQ both times κύριος
	ix. 6	י׳ alone, B κύριος παντοκράτωρ, AQ κύριος ὁ θεὸς ὁ παντοκράτωρ

The table in the footnote on p. 126 shews that of the seven passages where ⁙ 'אֲ is used in connection with the two formulae

κύριος κύριος in B occurs 3 times, κύριος ὁ θεός occurs 3 times and κύριος once;

κύριος κύριος in A occurs twice, κύριος ὁ θεός occurs 4 times and κύριος once;

κύριος κύριος in Q occurs once, κύριος ὁ θεός occurs 5 times and κύριος once.

If we are right in thinking that κύριος ὁ θεός is the equivalent of the Masoretic pronunciation and that it is a later rendering than κύριος κύριος, then only four passages witness to an earlier text. Two κύριος κύριος are represented in an Old Latin MS. (Weingartensis) by simple 'dominus', while in the third passage the Old Latin is wanting; and thus the possibility is suggested that in all the seven cases the original reading was simple κύριος.

The phenomena in Isaiah are on similar lines.* The LXX confirms the double name by reading in B three κύριος κύριος (xxviii. 16, xxx. 15, lii. 4), but B also five times reads κύριος

*	**ISAIAH** (see pp. 129 f.)
i–xxxix:	B*
5 ⁙ 'אֲ with כה אמר	vii. 7 κύριος σαβαώθ
	xxviii. 16 κύριος κύριος, אAQ* κύριος
	xxx. 15 κύριος κύριος, אA κύριος
'אֲ ⁙ צבאות	x. 24 κύριος σαβαώθ, א*ΑΓ κύριος ὁ θεός
	xxii. 15 κύριος σαβαώθ, אQ^{mg} κύριος κύριος
1 ⁙ 'אֲ with נאם	iii. 15 omits, Q^{mg}※ φησὶ κύριος κύριος (πιπι πιπι)
xl–lxvi:	
3 ⁙ 'אֲ with כה אמר	xlix. 22 κύριος B^{ab}Q^{mg} κύριος κύριος
	lii. 4 κύριος κύριος, אAQ κύριος
	lxv. 13 κύριος, Q^{mg} σ'θ'※ κύριος κύριος
1 ⁙ 'אֲ with נאם	lvi. 8 κύριος, Q^{mg} κύριος κύριος

With neither formula: 6 in i–xxxix (5 followed by צבאות), 10 in xl–lxvi (with no additions).

(x. 24, xxii. 15, xlix. 22, lxv. 13, lvi. 8; σαβαώθ being the translation in the first two passages for צבאות) and in lii. 4 אAQ reads
κύριος. In iii. 15 the Divine name is omitted altogether and
once κύριος σαβαώθ is for the double name (vii. 7).

Jeremiah (see p. 110) in MT has א' 'י five times in connection
with the same two formulae, out of 14 total uses (five being
in the vocative). Here again, out of five uses above-mentioned
only one is confirmed by LXX (B), two by A, and these by
κύριος ὁ θεός, which seems to be the equivalent of the MT
pronunciation and therefore late. In the other four passages
simple κύριος is found.*

Obadiah supplies us with the last example among 'the
Prophets' of the double name with one of the two formulae.†
Obadiah belongs to a late period and it is not unlikely that
the translation is later than that of other prophets. Perhaps,
as in Ezekiel xl–xlviii, so here, the translator read the א' 'י
as it now stands in MT and reproduced the pronunciation
'Adonai Elohim', which had by that time become customary.

Taking the Hebrew and the LXX occurrences together, the
most probable explanation seems to be that Editorial hands
first introduced the א' before 'י in the passages where it occurs
with the two formulae, and that its use spread from there
into other passages where it was desired to speak with special
solemnity. This is exclusive of the vocatival use of א' 'י which
we have found reason to believe belongs to the original LXX.

That Editors or copyists have made changes in the Hebrew

* 1 'י א' with כה אמר   vii. 20 BאAQ κύριος
  1 'י א' with נאם   ii. 22 BאQ κύριος, A κύριος ὁ θεός σου
  3 צבאות 'י א' with נאם ii. 19 BאAQ κύριος ὁ θεός σου
     (one line above LXX has the same Greek for אֱלֹהֶיךָ 'י)
                          xlix. (xxx) 5 BאAQ κύριος
                          l (xxvii) 31 BאAQ κύριος

† Verse 1 'י א' כה אמר, BאAQ all read τάδε λέγει κύριος ὁ θεός;
Sangallensis reads 'dominus deus'.

text after the birth of the LXX seems clear from a comparison
of 1 and 2 Esdras and Greek Chronicles. It is generally agreed
that 1 Esdras i. 1–ii. 5 is an earlier and an independent translation of the Hebrew of 2 Chron. xxxv. 1–xxxvi. 22. If these
two translations be compared, it will be seen that in several
places 1 Esdras has κύριος, where the Greek 2 Chronicles has
θεός (2 Chron. xxxv. 21, 22, xxxvi. 18, 22 with 1 Esdras i. 25,
26, 49, ii. 5), answering to the אלהים of MT, and we conclude
that the Hebrew text before the translator of 1 Esdras had יי
and that this had been changed into אלהים by the time that
the translation in 2 Chronicles was made. In 2 Esdras the
process seems to have gone still further. For example, take
Ezra viii. 17–25. The corresponding passage in 1 Esdras
viii. 45–53 translates five times (τοῦ) κυρίου ἡμῶν, whereas
2 Esdras viii. 17–25 translates θεοῦ ἡμῶν in conformity with
the אלהים of the present Hebrew text (cf. Ezra ix. 4–6, 1 Esdras
viii. 69–71, 2 Esdras ix. 4–6, etc., etc.). 2 Esdras moreover in
16 places where MT has יי does not express it in the Greek
(e.g. Neh. viii. 1, 10, x. 35 f., etc.).

It would be a mistake, however, to say that the change in
these cases is due to deliberate purpose on the part of Editors
of the Hebrew text to avoid the pronunciation of the Sacred
name יי. In Chronicles, for example, יי occurs 543 times
(175 in 1 Chron., 368 in 2 Chron.) in MT. There is no such
wholesale change as is to be seen in the Elohistic Psalms.
אלהים occurs in MT 143 times (63 in 1 Chron., 80 in 2 Chron.).
The corresponding θεός occurs only 100 times (54 in 1 Chron.,
46 in 2 Chron.), κύριος taking its place some 38 times. Further,
there are on the one hand 23 omissions of יי in the translation
and on the other hand nine uses of κύριος where the Divine
name is not expressed in the Hebrew.

Again, if Chronicles be compared with Kings, we see that
Kings has 'house of יי' 70 times and never has 'house of אלהים'.

Chronicles reads 'house of ה׳' 68 times but also 'house of אלהים'
31 times (11 times in 1 Chron., 20 in 2 Chron.). In the passages
which are common to both, in at least 15 cases 'house of ה׳'
in Kings is replaced by 'house of God' in Chronicles. In like
manner 'the ark of ה׳' is used in Chronicles five times (1 Chron.
xv. 3, 12, 14, xvi. 4; 2 Chron. viii. 11) but 'ark of God' occurs
twelve times (1 Chron. xiii. 5 ff., 12, 14, xv. 1 f. twice, 15, 24,
xvi. 1; 2 Chron. i. 4). The explanation would seem to be that
the later Jews came to speak of 'house of God' and 'the ark of
God', etc. rather than of the 'house of ה׳' or 'the ark of ה׳', and
that in consequence, even when they incorporated passages
from Samuel and Kings, they instinctively used the forms of
expression which had by their time become habitual.

Finally, in the Kᵉthuvim ה׳ אֵ׳ only occurs four times, all
four being in the Psalms. The inverted אֵ׳ ה׳ also occurs four
times, all in the Psalms. A fifth case occurs in the Book
of the Prophet Habakkuk (iii. 19). In all probability Hab. iii
is itself a Psalm, taken out of a collection of Psalms. It may
have been joined on to the prophecies of Habakkuk at a very
late date. The LXX rendering in Habakkuk points to such
a proceeding (κύριος ὁ θεός). It may be added that the translator of Psalm lxxi. 16, whether original translator or Editor,
regarded the אֵ׳ there as a proper name. Six of the nine
occurrences are in the vocative (see p. 104, note §).

III. Our study of the LXX translations of the Hebrew
original, in the places where the double Divine name occurs
in the MT, has led us to doubt whether, as a rule at any rate,
the אֵ׳ before ה׳ (apart from its use in the vocative) lay before
the original translators. A similar study of the LXX in places
where in the MT a written אֵ׳ stands alone is indecisive,
because the κύριος standing in these places could equally well
represent an original ה׳.

Let us approach the question now from another side. At first sight it may seem obvious that the use of κύριος in the Greek text for the ⁀ of the Hebrew text must have arisen from the use of 'א in the public reading of the Scriptures in the Synagogue as the spoken substitute for the Sacred name.

But was that the case? When did this pronunciation come in? It is now argued that this use, and still more the written use of 'א as a proper name, did not come in before 100 B.C. at the earliest. If that can be proved, then clearly the choice of κύριος, instead of a literal translation or transliteration of the Sacred name, is independent of the pronunciation adopted in Synagogue reading, because that only came in after the earliest translation of the LXX was made.

To this question we must therefore now address ourselves. When did this Synagogal use come in?

1. κύριος was from the first used as substitute for ⁀ by the LXX.

(i) Origen in his Commentary on Psalm ii remarks that 'in the most accurate of the copies (ἀντίγραφα) the name is given in Hebrew characters—characters not as now but the most ancient'. Jerome and others understood this as referring to the earliest MSS. of the LXX and as shewing that not κύριος at first but a transcription in Hebrew letters was used. In that case κύριος would come later and not be part of the original LXX. But by 'the most accurate copies' Origen was in all probability actually referring, not to the LXX, but to the translations of Aquila and Symmachus, which date from the second century A.D. Fragments of these later translations are extant in quotations by Church Fathers which shew the tetragrammaton written in the ancient Hebrew characters as πιπι, which to Greek copyists would naturally be read from left to right as πιπι and was consequently so written. Theodotion held to the older LXX translators and only emended their phrasing, and he apparently always uses κύριος for ⁊. And Aquila seems to have regarded κύριος as the pronunciation of his יחוה with Hebrew characters, as he once so abbreviated the ⁊. Origen therefore does not state anything which militates against the use of κύριος by the LXX from the first.

(ii) What testimony we have as to the usage of the LXX in regard to the Divine name is all relatively late. The letter of Aristeas says that Moses in the Scripture said μνείᾳ μνησθήσῃ κυρίου τοῦ [θεοῦ]. κύριος is only used in this one passage and in it it is used of Holy Scripture. This seems clearly to give us the LXX usage. Philo certainly found κύριος in his LXX text. 'Wisdom' uses Κύριος as a proper name without article, seemingly for ⁊. 2 and 3 Maccabees also so use κύριος.

(iii) The use of κύριος for ⁊ in the LXX also seems to be independent of the Synagogue-pronunciation for the following reasons:

(a) ⁊ 'א is translated by δέσποτα κύριε twice in Genesis and twice in Jeremiah, thus distinguishing between ⁊ and 'א and not translating by κύριε κύριε as later translators did.

(b) The use of κύριος as a rule without the article, not only in the nominative, but also in the genitive, dative and accusative, points in the same direction, for a ⁊ in Hebrew letters and therefore not inflected would not be intelligible.

(c) The use of κύριος in Isaiah, Psalms, Job and Ecclesiasticus as a rendering of אֵל and in Daniel O and 1 Esdras as a rendering of אֱלָה and other Divine names seems to shew that κύριος was not regarded as identified with the pronunciation of ⁊ as though it were 'א, but rather as having become so much *the* Divine name that it could be used for other Divine names as well as for ⁊.

2. The use of אדני, in passages where it is now represented by κύριος, is twofold.

(i) In the Pentateuch it is used only in the vocative. Num.

xiv. 17 is in all probability a corruption of the Text (p. 106). In these cases it may therefore be taken as = my Lord. But in the Former and Later Prophets and the Keᵉthuvim in most cases it is clearly used as = the Lord, although Dalman has argued that, with very few exceptions which he puts down to copyists' errors, 'א is everywhere = 'my Lord'. The pronominal suffix has clearly lost its significance. In the Former Prophets the only passages where the signification 'my Lord' is suitable are in the vocative. In the Later Prophets and in the Psalms individuals speak, but as a rule they speak of the relation of the people to Jehovah, not of their own personal relationship. אלהים with the suffix of the first person singular is very rare in the older Scriptures, whereas in post-exilic Scriptures it occurs frequently. The use of 'א as vocative and in address to God in the third person in the mouth of individuals (as e.g. Gen. xviii. 27, 30 ff., Exod. xxxiv. 9) is then clearly ancient. Quite possibly the form used correctly from of old in address to God lost its original force and came to be used outside such address, but, if so, such usage is probably not of high antiquity, seeing that the pronominal suffix retains its force in the early use to a relatively late period (as in Psalms xxxv. 23, xxxviii. 16, lxxxvi. 12).*

The loss of the significance of the pronominal suffix is ob-

---

* It is true that Lagarde and 'Bauer and Leander' have both attempted to shew that the '־ of אֲדֹנָי is an Aramaic or Canaanitish noun-ending, but we know no pre-Semitic language to which this noun-ending may belong, and it would be a very surprising fact if only in Hebrew has the original form survived. Since in Phoenician, as in Hebrew, the title אָדוֹן is clearly used of God with pronominal suffix, that seems the most probable explanation of אֲדֹנִי. The use of pronominal suffixes with the Divine name to indicate that the God belongs to his worshippers is found in Babylonian, Phoenician, Aramaean and South Arabian and is clearly an ancient usage, characteristic of Semitic religion.

servable in many languages, e.g. Rabbi, Monsieur, Madonna. אֲדֹנִי, used in address to man (as e.g. 2 Sam. xviii. 28 'my lord the King' and 1 Kings i. 43, 47 'our lord the King'), never lost the significance of the suffix, but אֲדֹנָי, used of God, when not in vocative, has lost the pronominal significance as e.g. in 1 Kings iii. 10, where we read that Solomon's words were good in the eyes of אֲדֹנָי and, in some texts, in verse 15 'the ark of the covenant of אֲדֹנָי' (variant יהוה).

In like manner אֲ יְ has lost in most cases the significance of the suffix. The אֲ is not a title placed before the proper Divine name, but has become an integral part of a compound Divine name, and the question is: When did this use as a proper name come in, and by whom was it so used (original author or Editor)?

(ii) It is in Malachi (iii. 1) that for the first time we find Jehovah spoken of as הָאָדֹון, and then only in a figure. It is the son of Sirach who first uses אָדֹון as a name for Jehovah. Before him אָדֹון (κύριος) without article and standing alone is never found as a Divine name nor is it ever used as a predicate to express how a man thought of God. So long as this was the usage of אדון, אדֹני cannot well be taken as a name of Jehovah. Certainly not before Malachi. Although we do find such a usage in the Masoretic text of the Old Testament and this forms a basis of the later usage in the Targums, the Synagogue and Judaism generally, it would seem that the use of אדֹני as a Divine proper name did not arise out of the living speech of the people in Old Testament times, but rather resulted from its deliberate adoption by the Scribes after the epoch of Old Testament literature had ended.

When then did this usage begin? It is reasonable to take it that it arose from the growing timidity of readers to employ the Sacred name in public speech. As early as Deuteronomy (xxviii. 58) observance of the Law is associated with the fear of 'this glorious and fearful name, Jehovah thy God'. And the growth of a universal idea of God may early have led to the use of a general Divine name instead of a particularist name. In any case later Judaism feared to pronounce, not to write, the Sacred name. Josephus refers to the fear lest it should be degraded by its pronunciation in the mouth of non-Jews. This would be avoided if another pronunciation were adopted in the public reading. Once this habit had come in, it was inevitable that copyists, especially if writing from dictation, would sometimes write 'א for 'י and, later on, it is easily conceivable that Editors would at times use it independently of any pre-existing 'י.

(iii) This relation of the written to the merely spoken 'א seems to lie behind the usage of 'א and 'י 'א in definite groups of books.* We seem to see four definite stages.

In the Pentateuch אדני as a Divine name is used only in address to God.

In the Former Prophets 'א in reported speech occurs rarely, 'י 'א only once. In Joshua and Judges the two are both used only in address to God. In 1 Samuel neither is used. In 2 Samuel 'א is not found and 'י 'א is used only in address to God. In 1 and 2 Kings the two are found six times, once in the vocative, five times in narrative.

In the Later Prophets the usage is quite different. The occurrences (282 of the double name, 37 of 'א alone) are far too numerous to be explained as copyists' errors. Some other factor is clearly at work.

In the Kᵉthuvim the double name only occurs eight times and the 'א is almost entirely confined to the Psalms and Lamentations. In Chronicles, five minor prophets (including Hosea), Proverbs, Canticles, Ruth, Ecclesiastes and Esther both are entirely absent.

* See Table III (p. 152) and see the lists of passages on pp. 104 f.

Taking these four groups in turn, it would appear that, at the time when 'א as the public pronunciation for 'י came in, the Pentateuch was already sacrosanct and was copied with careful accuracy. In the Former Prophets the examples of 'א in reported speech, and the one example of 'י 'א, are few and are confined to 1 and 2 Kings. In five out of the six we find a variant 'י and text-corruption is always possible. It may well be that originally in the Former Prophets the use of 'א and of 'י 'א as proper names was entirely absent.

The usage in the Later Prophets cannot be explained in a similar manner. The use of 'א and 'י 'א in the vocative is now rare (only 15), while that in narrative is very numerous (304). If we are right in thinking that the earlier use was confined to the vocative and to the address to God in the third person singular and that the use in narrative only came in after the completion of the original writings of the Old Testament (p. 134), then we must conclude that during the period after the canonization of the Law and before the canonization of the Prophetic writings later Editors introduced this name 'א, and equally the double name, into prophetic speech deliberately, in order to emphasize a special aspect of the Divine Being.

Finally comes the group, represented by Chronicles and other late writings, which made no use of 'א at all. These writings were not publicly read in the Synagogue at the time when the second and third divisions of the Canon were put together. It may therefore be supposed that the Sacred name could in private use still be pronounced as it was written, and that, by the time that these books were admitted into the Canon, greater care was bestowed upon the copying, and 'א would not be written for 'י.*

* Compare the use of the name Baal. This name for an idol was also latterly not pronounced in the public reading in the Synagogue,

We note that even the vocatival אֲ is absent from Chronicles and also (with the exception of 1 Kings viii. 53) from Kings. As a matter of fact it occurs relatively seldom in the Old Testament as a whole and chiefly in the oldest narratives (the Pentateuch, Joshua and Judges). Among the Prophets perhaps only Isaiah uses it and that only two or three times. It was clearly an old form of speech which lingered on in lyrical and liturgical speech (Psalms, the prayer in Dan. ix, and once each in Lam. iii. 58 and in the prayer in Neh. i. 11), but otherwise died out. This would explain its absence from Chronicles. The absence of אֲ יי is more striking, because that occurs seven times in 2 Sam. vii. 1 and 1 Kings viii. 53, which Chronicles incorporated in its narrative. It must have been intentionally evaded by the later writer and either יי (3) אלהים (1) or יי אלהים (3) substituted in its place. Among the other 'Writings' only in Psalms (17) and Lamentations (13 or 14) is אֲ frequently used in non-vocational speech (see p. 152) and only in Psalms does יי אֲ or אֲ יי occur (4 or 3) in narrative. These were probably the earliest of the 'Writings' to be regarded

in order that the congregation might not be defiled by its use, and the word 'Bosheth' (the shameful thing) was substituted for it (Jer. iii. 24, xi. 13, Hos. ix. 10). The LXX witnesses to this as coming in early, by its ἡ αἰσχύνη in 1 Kings xviii. 19 and by its use of the article in the feminine ἡ Βάαλ in Jer. ii. 8 (+ 10 times), Hosea, etc. (cf. Rom. xi. 4), although more often ὁ Βάαλ is found (Judges, 2 Samuel, Kings, etc.). So also in 1 and 2 Kings we find the personal names Ishbosheth, Mephibosheth, etc., whereas in Chronicles, which was not used in public reading, the original Ishbaal, Meribbaal, etc., are retained. But it is a question whether the original translators of the LXX knew of this use, for as a rule it retains Baal. That seems to witness to a later change in the Hebrew text and a partial editing of the LXX text in Kings and Prophets in accordance therewith, while the latest books, when they came to be regarded as Holy Scriptures, were admitted without their text being conformed to the new method.

as Canonical, and therefore the same tendency to substitute 'אֲ
for אֲ is observable as in the Later Prophets. The absence of both
'אֲ and אֲ 'אֲ in the other 'Writings' is then to be explained on
the same lines as in Chronicles.

3. Can we find reliable evidence outside the LXX as to
when 'אֲ came to be written in the Hebrew text, or at least
spoken by the public reader in the Synagogue?

(i) Aquila, Symmachus and Theodotion are pre-Hexaplaric.
Aquila once, and Symmachus repeatedly, translate 'אֲ in the
vocative by δέσποτα, but as a rule Aquila has κύριος. Theodotion
uniformly renders κύριος. Knowledge of 'אֲ as a proper name
cannot be definitely proved, but perhaps for all three it can
be inferred, as they knew the double אֲ 'אֲ, which they translate
in three different ways: Ἀδωναί κύριος (or Ἀδωναί πιπι), κύριος
κύριος and κύριος ὁ θεός (or πιπι ὁ θεός). This gives evidence for
the double name as far back as the first half of the second
century A.D.*

(ii) The Targums, Samaritan Targums and Peshito are
early in origin, but in their present form are late and we
cannot therefore rely upon their evidence. The earliest witness
is really the Old Latin ('Dominus Deus') in Ezekiel xl–xlviii
(see pp. 119–121).

(iii) Origen gives the first clearly dated witness for the
pronunciation of the Sacred name by 'אֲ in public reading.
In his comment on Psalm ii he definitely states that the Jews
pronounced the tetragrammaton ἀδωναί. He also witnesses six
times to the use of 'אֲ in place of אֲ in the Hebrew text which

---

* Von Baudissin doubts whether Aquila and Theodotion have
been correctly reported by the Christian writers who quote extracts
from them. He thinks that those who report their rendering may
have found in their MSS. πιπι in the text and a note Ἀδωναί in the
margin and that they read these two together as a double name and
expressed them in the Greek form familiar to them. So in Amos vii. 7
Theodotion has ἀδωναί κύριος, where MT has simple אֲ.

he gives in the first column of the Hexapla. He therefore certainly read 'א as a proper name.*

4. While Origen gives us the earliest clear date of the use of 'א as proper name, the actual use can be much earlier than the extant witnesses.

(i) We have already referred to the tendency to avoid the writing of the Sacred name. The Elohistic Psalms seem to exhibit this tendency, which would bring us to the middle of the third century B.C. The LXX translators of the Psalms generally (although not always or without MS. variation) translate אלהים by θεός and יהוה by κύριος in accordance with MT. Although the LXX translation of the Psalms belongs to the later time, yet in its usage in respect of the Divine names it is in harmony with the oldest translations. This would carry us back to the middle of the third century B.C. and form the first example of the tendency to avoid the written name.

Chronicles in Greek is much later. As we have seen (pp. 129 f.) there appears to be a tendency to prefer אלהים or האלהים. The present MT of Chronicles seems to point to a further carrying out of the process after the LXX translation had been made. The author of Qoheleth exclusively uses אלהים (probably as not specifically Israelite) and so do Esther (where we find 'another place' used as substitute for the Sacred name) and 1 Maccabees (Heaven). Daniel employs other general Divine names, except in the prayer of chapter ix, which is clearly of later origin than the rest of the Book. The use of יהוה in chapter ix shews that in prayer-speech it was still allowable to use and write the name. Clearly there was

---

* All the Greek names used in the Apocrypha and the Pseudepigrapha, which can possibly be regarded as witnesses to an 'א as proper name, either spoken or written, fall in a time so much later than the date of the original translators of the LXX that they may reasonably be held to have arisen after that date.

variety of view on the subject for a long time. But the use of אלהים at times instead of ׳י shews that it was not the regular custom to substitute א׳. א׳ is used in Dan. ix alongside ׳י in MT, but it may be questioned whether this use is original.

(ii) Further, we have definite statements that the pronunciation of the Sacred name was avoided and that another name was substituted.

Philo affords us the first datable statement on this point. He speaks of a long-existing timidity as to the pronouncing of an unspecified Divine name. He speaks of the 'four letters' as engraved on the High Priest's diadem and of a secret name pronounced only ἐν ἁγίοις. He uses the κύριος of the LXX regularly himself, but we cannot be sure from his somewhat conflicting statements what he thought to be the relation between this κύριος and the 'four letters', or whether he knew anything definite as to the proper pronunciation of the secret name or as to its substitute. For Philo there was (a) no real name of God. He is above all naming; (b) a secret name only spoken ἐν ἁγίοις, and (c) the 'four letters' which signifies this Sacred name and is identical with κύριος.*

Josephus says that it was not permissible for him to speak about the name announced to Moses, and he adds that he had had to use a neutral substitute in order to avoid it, but he does not say whether this substitute was a generally accepted one or not.

The statements in the Talmuds are conflicting and they come from a time after the downfall of the Temple. The

---

* Ewald, Kittel, Dillmann and others have held that the pronunciation of א׳ for ׳י was dominant in the time of Philo, but this rests on the supposition that the κύριος of the LXX is a *translation* of the spoken א׳. Von Baudissin disputes this view. It is, he says, just this point which is in question, and Philo does not state that this was the case (*Kyrios*, II. Teil, VII. K.).

Mishna (Sota vii. 6, Tamid vii. 2) states that in the case of the Priestly benediction 'in the Temple they say *the Name* as it is written and in the Country [Synagogues] according to its naming (בְּכִנּוּיוֹ)'. Undoubtedly this latter meant the pronunciation 'אֲ, which was by this time the sole recognized substitute. But this statement would not apply to the period before the destruction of the Temple, as the Priestly benediction was not dispensed otherwise than in the Temple. The Synagogue service was confined to the reading and exposition of Scripture by scribes and lawyers. The Mishna statement therefore seems to mean that after the cessation of the Temple worship the pronunciation of the Sacred name came to be generally inhibited and just at that time its replacement by 'אֲ came in. In public reading the Sacred name had either to be pronounced or a substitute used. Though neither Philo nor Josephus nor any other witness definitely says that the substitute was 'אֲ, yet we know of no other ever used in this way, nor can it have come suddenly after the cessation of the Temple worship. The Mishna certainly speaks as if it were a custom already in existence at that time. And as Chronicles was not definitely recognized as Holy Scripture until the Synod of Jamnia (about A.D. 90), and as the absence of 'אֲ in Chronicles probably means that the natural pronunciation of 'י was still retained in non-Canonical books, which were read in private, it is probable that the pronunciation by 'אֲ was in use in the public reading of Canonical Scriptures.

If the statements about the renderings by Aquila and Symmachus are to be trusted and if the written 'אֲ in Old Testament Texts (apart from vocatival use) arose at first out of copyists' errors (due to the pronunciation in the public reading) and if then Editorial revisers added an 'אֲ to the originally simple 'י, considerable time must be allowed for the process. Perhaps, however, a century is long enough. If so, we need not go further back than 100 B.C. for the beginning of the process. This use in the public reading would inevitably in time affect the private speech of the people, but the process would only slowly take effect.

(iii) Indications of the gradual passing away of the proper pronunciation of ˙ are preserved in ancient writings. It is clear that the old pronunciation, partly in full form, partly in popular shortened form, survived at least into the second century A.D. in circles outside the Synagogues.

(a) In the Judaic literature after the Old Testament we can trace the natural pronunciation of ˙ up to Daniel (chapter ix) and to Sirach (l. 20f., where he describes the blessing of the congregation in the Temple in the name of κύριος by Simon, son of Onias, the High Priest). Probably the κύριος of the Apocrypha and Pseudepigrapha points to the same use. 4 Esdras and the Syriac Baruch with their 'dominator domine' (which seems to be equivalent to δέσποτα κύριε) point to an ˙ ´א in the vocative, pronounced according to their natural sound.

(b) In the Elephantine papyri (fifth century B.C.) we find יהו, which corresponds to the Jahu or Jĕhō in Old Testament proper names, and the military colony there must have brought it with them in the pre-Persian period (seventh century B.C.). We find the same shortened name on coins of the fifth and fourth centuries B.C.

(c) 'Ιαώ as the name of a Deity occurs over and over again in documents of very varied origin. Taking only cases where the context clearly refers to the God of the Jews, we note the following in accounts given us of pre-Christian and later non-Christian Greek and Roman writings: Marcus T. Varro, the Roman man of letters (116–27 B.C.), refers to the name 'Ιαώ as Chaldaean. Diodorus Siculus (living in the days of Caesar and Augustus) in his picture of Egypt speaks of the God of

Moses as Ἰαώ. Philo Byblius, cited by Lydus (sixth century), speaks of Ἰαώ and tells Old Testament stories (not directly taken from the Old Testament). Eusebius says that Sanchuniathos, whose writings Philo Byblius had translated into Greek, had received his information from a history written by a priest of the God Ἰευώ (clearly = Yahweh) and that this priest lived near the time of Moses.

(d) The Divine name Ἰαώ is found in magical writings; Ἰαώ and Ἰευ in Gnostic writings and in the Oracle of Apollo Clarius. In the second century A.D. Ἰαώ is found on gems and magical papyri from districts which are wide apart. So are Ἀδωναί and Σαβαώθ (the latter is found 69 times with Ἰαώ, and 20 times with Ἀδωναί). Ἀδωναί as a rule is an epithet of Ἰαώ. The name of Ἰαώ is regarded as powerful in oaths and he is called 'the God of Abraham and of Isaac and of Σαβαώθ'. The name is found on phylacteries as protecting against fiends. The Gnostics also used the popular form, the Jews apparently either not knowing or not daring to use the full form. They also use Adoneus as the name for a special demon or god distinct from Ἰαώ.

In the Coptic Pistis Sophia Ἰαώ and Ἰευ played a great role, and the older Coptic Gnostic Apocryphon of John used the name Ἀδωναῖος.

The Oracle of Apollo in Claros names Ἰαώ as the highest of all gods and identifies him with Hades, Zeus and Helios.

(e) In early Christian literature we find transcriptions. Irenaeus gives Ἰαώθ, obtained probably from popular speech. Clement of Alexandria gives Ἰαουέ, learnt from a Jewish scribe, as the pronunciation in the days when it was written on the High Priest's clothing. Origen nowhere says how the tetragrammaton was pronounced. He only says that ἀδωναί was pronounced instead. He retained in Exodus the Hebrew letters. He says that Ἰαώ was used by the Gnostics, but not

that it was used in his day. He gives Ἰά as the Hebrew pronunciation (i.e. יָהּ), as did Theodotion. Jerome says that the
name of God among the Hebrews has four letters, but that
it was not to be pronounced, being 'ineffable'. Clearly he did
not himself know how to pronounce it. Theodoret says the
Samaritans pronounced the Sacred name Ἰαβέ. In a list of
Divine names he puts ἀδωναί before Ἐλωί and Σαβαώθ, which
suggests that his informant gave that pronunciation to the
tetragrammaton. Epiphanius gave Ἰαβέ as one among several
Hebrew Divine names, including Sabaoth and Rabboni, which
are all (with the exception of Rabboni) of Old Testament
character and says that all are designations of the One God.

From the fourth century onwards the witness is all secondary.
Rabbinic threatenings against the pronunciation of the tetragrammaton in the second century A.D. shew that so far the
true pronunciation was not uncustomary. First the full form
and then the popular form came to be regarded as too dan-
gerous. Till then the official pronunciation had not completely
conquered. The witness of Varro and later writers to the use
of Ἰαώ in the mouths of the people, at a time when ׳א had
come to be used in the Synagogues, indicates that at the time
when the LXX was originally translated (i.e. three or four
centuries earlier) the official pronunciation, ׳א = κύριος, cannot
have been the usual one.

But we have not yet reached a definite date at which it was
introduced. It is 700 years from the Elohistic Psalms to the
full sway of the pronunciation by ׳א in place of ׳י in the fourth
century A.D. It is no wonder that in this slow evolution particular changes can only be vaguely delimited. If we may put
the Synagogue rule as coming in between 100 B.C. and A.D. 100,
then the κύριος of the earliest LXX was not a rendering of
an ׳א spoken for ׳י nor of a written ׳א used as a proper
name. The first translator who seems to have read ׳א in his

Hebrew exemplar would be the translator of Ezek. xl–xlviii, and he will not have done his work before 100 B.C.

5. But if κύριος is not a translation of the substituted 'א, what is the relation between the two? May not the choice both of 'א in the Hebrew text and of κύριος in the LXX have been more or less independently made, resting on a common need?

(i) The motive for the choice of κύριος as the substitute for the Sacred name in the LXX may well be traced to the feeling that merely to transliterate the tetragrammaton (assuming that they knew its proper pronunciation) would have suggested that their God was only one among other Gods. The developed monotheism of the Alexandrian Jews regarded a proper name as not appropriate to the One God. They therefore chose an appellative instead, and thus they repudiated the idea which may be seen in the usage of the Elephantine papyri, viz. of יְהוּ as one among other Gods. κύριος then is neither transliteration nor translation, but substitute.

(ii) But why κύριος? We may see an indication of the reason for this if we note the use of κύριος in the LXX, outside its employment for ', in cases where it does not occur as a Divine name, but as a translation of a Hebrew title.

(a) κύριος is the regular translation of אָדוֹן. As applied to men, this is always the case in the Pentateuch and generally so elsewhere. (Δεσπότης is twice used, in each case for obvious reasons, Josh. xv. 14, Prov. xxx. 10 (xxiv. 33).) As address to God, the case, with rare exceptions, is the same. Clearly the translators regard κύριος as the proper translation of אדן.

(b) אדן in the Old Testament, as used of God, has the sense of 'Lord'. Out of 86 examples of this word in the Pentateuch in reference to a man, 58 are vocatival, and the pronominal suffix in אדני always has full force, 'My Master' or 'Lord'. So, as applied to God in private prayer אדני always expresses the thought that the Lord specially belonged to His worshipper. In the Psalms it is used 27 times in the vocative, and the double name four or five times in the same way. P in the Pentateuch does not use it. P does not deal with private prayer. The Greek Esther, 1 Esdras and Ecclesiasticus shew that the Greek-speaking Jews of Egypt used κύριε in private prayer and therefore probably the oldest translators found this use ready to hand, when they had to translate אדני.

(c) In the older portions of the LXX κύριος has the force of 'Superior' rather than of Ruler, i.e. He to whom another person belongs, not necessarily he who rules over another. The use of κύριος as the Divine name corresponds to that of אדן as meaning One who belongs to the individual or the community.

(d) But also this use of κύριος corresponds in a measure to a use of κύριος as a Divine title by the non-Jewish nations around. In the middle of the first century B.C. κύριος occurs in such employment in numerous, widely sundered, witnesses as a formula which had clearly been long in use in the Near East. It seems to be a Grecizing of a widespread Divine predicate, signifying 'Lord', and probably came into use when Greek speech spread in the East in the time of Alexander the Great. κύριος, so employed, was not used of any one God by himself and was almost as universal as θεός. It is used of Gods in Egypt and in Syria. Only in monotheistic Judaism does it come to be used as a proper name. It may be taken that the Old Testament אדן and the Gentile κύριος combined to influence the oldest LXX translators, both having come from the same old-Canaanitish אדן.

(iii) If this be the motive for the choice of κύριος as substitute for י in the LXX, can we see also a similar motive for the choice of א by Palestinian revisers of the Hebrew text as the spoken substitute for י in the public reading of the Synagogue?

Although it would seem as if the κύριος came first, it does not follow that the spoken 'א is simply a translation of κύριος adopted from the LXX. If it were so, why do we find אדני and not אדן, which is the correct equivalent of κύριος? Moreover, the pride of the Palestinian scholars would make them loath to imitate the Alexandrians. It is reasonable to expect that the scribes would find in the Old Testament sacred text itself the justification of their choice of a substitute for 'י in Synagogal reading, even if they were also influenced by the LXX use. Intercourse of a kind between Egypt and Palestine was not wanting—witness the Elephantine letters and the letter of Aristeas. Philo knows how the tetragrammaton was treated at the Feasts in Jerusalem and at least once himself visited Jerusalem. This fellowship was never quite lost. The preface to Ecclesiasticus witnesses to literary intercourse. The late passage in Isa. xix. 18 makes honourable mention of the Temple at Heliopolis, according to the most probable reading. The letter prefixed to 2 Maccabees wishes well to the 'brethren' in Egypt and calls upon them to keep the Feast of Tabernacles. Above all, we note the high respect felt for the LXX in all Judaism and its general use by the Diaspora, until its use by Christians caused it to fall into disrepute among the strict Orthodox Jews.

The Palestinian scribes might well see in the κύριος of the LXX a finger-post for some analogous substitute in the public reading of their Hebrew Old Testament, and the אדני (in singular or plural), already in use as the traditional mode of address to God, would suggest that that should be the actual form of the substitute, the regular address in prayer having gradually lost the pronominal significance of its ending (as it did among later West Semites). While the impulse may have been received from the LXX κύριος, the Palestinians could regard the word they chose as independently taken from their

Hebrew Scriptures. The intercourse with Egypt was inter-
rupted, when Rome made Palestine a part of the province
of Syria, and the Christian use of the LXX caused a reaction
against it in orthodox Judaism. We may therefore conclude
that the use of 'א in the place of י probably came in some-
where near the beginning of the Christian era. The fact that
אדני is also a tetragrammaton may also have influenced the
use of it. The modification to אדֹנָי was probably adopted at
or about the same time in order to distinguish it from the
use to men.

TABLE I

Occurrences of the double Divine name in MT

Pentateuch	4	all in the vocative
Former Prophets	11	10 in the vocative
Later Prophets	282	217 being in Ezekiel, only 12 in address to God (2 Amos, 5 Jeremiah, 5 Ezekiel)
The 'Writings'	8	half being in address to God
Total	305	

Occurrences of 'Adonai' standing alone

Pentateuch	14	13 in address to God (Num. xiv. 17 also in LXX)
Former Prophets	8	3 (Josh. and Judg.) in address to God
		5 (1 and 2 Kings) otherwise
Later Prophets	37	only 3 in address to God
The 'Writings'	78	39 in address to God (29 in Psalms, 8 in Dan. ix; 1 each in Lamentations and Nehemiah)
Total	137	

אדני otherwise than in address occurs in Isaiah 21 times, Psalms 17 and Lamentations 15. Elsewhere its use is sporadic, Ezekiel 4 times in the mouth of the people, Amos 4, Micah and Zechariah once each, Malachi twice (or once). In the 'Writings' Job once, Daniel 4 times, Ezra–Nehemiah 1 or 2.

TABLE II

LXX renderings of the double Divine name

Pentateuch

Gen. xv. 2, 8	δέσποτα κύριε
Deut. iii. 24	κύριε ὁ θεός B, Boh., κύριε κύριε all other MSS. and versions
Deut. ix. 26	κύριε βασιλεῦ τῶν θεῶν Bᵃ₂ Eth., κύριε κύριε AFGMNΘ rel. Boh. and Lʳ Phil.; Domine Domine Deus Lat.ᶻ + Deus Arm.-codd.

Former Prophets

κύριέ μου κύριε	5
κύριέ μου	1
κύριε κύριε	1
ἀδωναιὲ κύριε	1
κύριε	2
κυρίου	1

Later Prophets	B	A and almost always ℵ and Q*

Isa. i–lxvi

κύριος κύριος	10	0
κύριος ὁ θεός	1	2 (+ 1 ὁ θεός alone)
κύριος Σαβαώθ	1	1
κύριος	11	19
omitted	2	2
	25	25

Isa. i–xxxix

κύριος	6	8
κύριος Σαβαώθ	1	1
κύριος κύριος	3	0
κύριος ὁ θεός	1	2 ὁ θεός alone
omitted	1	1
	12	12

Isa. xl–lxvi

	B*	Bᵃᵇ	ℵAQ*
κύριος κύριος	7	9	0
κύριος	6	4	13
	13	13	13

TABLE II (*continued*)

Jeremiah	B	A
In vocative 5		
δέσποτα κύριε	2	3
κύριε	2	
κύριε κύριε		1 (AQ)
Omit	1	1
Not in vocative 9		
κύριος	6	3
κύριος κύριος	0	1 (אAQ)
κύριος σαβαώθ	0	1
κύριος ὁ θεός σού} and κύριος ὁ θεὸς ἡμῶν}	2	3
τῷ κυρίῳ θεῷ	1	τῷ κυρίῳ 1 (A and Q)
	14	14
Amos		
In vocative 2		
κύριε	1	
κύριε κύριε	1	2
Not in vocative 19		
κύριος	7	7
κύριος κύριος	4	3
κύριος ὁ θεός	7	8
κύριος κύριος ὁ θεός	1	1
	21	21

Rest of Minor Prophets

Micah κύριος κύριος 1   κύριος 1 AQ* (κύριος ὁ θεός Qᵐᵍ)

Obadiah κύριος ὁ θεός 1   1

Zephaniah κύριου τοῦ θεοῦ 1   1

Zechariah κύριος παντο- 1   1 (verse 15 same for κράτωρ   צבאות י׳)

TABLE III

Adonai and Adonai Yahweh in and out of address to God.

Books	Adonai		AY or YA	
	in address	not in address	in address	not in address
Pentateuch	13 (? 14)	1 (? none)	4	—
Joshua	1	—	1	—
Judges	2	—	2	—
2 Samuel	—	—	6	—
1 Kings	—	3	1	1
2 Kings	—	2	—	—
Isaiah	3	21	—	25
Jeremiah	—	—	5	9
Ezekiel	—	5	5	212
Amos	—	4	2	19
Obadiah	—	—	—	1
Micah	—	1	—	1
Habakkuk	—	—	—	1 (YA)
Zephaniah	—	—	—	1
Zechariah	—	1	—	1
Malachi	—	2	—	—
Psalms	29	17	4 or 5 (3 YA)	4 or 3 (1 YA)
Job	—	1	—	—
Lamentations	1	13 or 14	—	—
Daniel	8	4	—	—
Ezra, Neh.	1	1	—	—
Hosea, Joel, Jonah, Nahum, Haggai, Chronicles, Proverbs, Canticles, Ruth, Ecclesiastes, Esther: no occurrences at all				
Totals	58 (59)	76 (77)	30 (or 31)	275 (274)

TABLE IV

Giving all the passages in which י׳ א׳ occurs in Ezekiel MT

(The second column indicates the phrase in which it occurs)

* = original hand; a, b, c = later hands; v = Lucianic readings

MT		B	A	Q
ii. 4	כה	κ	κκ	κκ
iii. 11	כה	κ	κκ	κκ
27	כה	κ	κκ	{ακ* / κκ^mg}
iv. 14	אהה	κθτl	κκθτl	{κθτl* / κοθτl^mg}
v. 5	כה	κ	ακ^v	ακ
7	כה	κ	ακ^v	ακ
8	כה	κ	ακ	ακ
11	נאם	κ	ακ	ακ
vi. 3a	דברי	κ	{κ* / ακ^a}	ακ
3b	כה	κ	ακ	ακ
11	כה	κ	ακ	ακ
vii. 2	כה	κ	ακ^v	ακ
5	כה	κ	κ	ακ
viii. 1	יד׳ו	κ	ακ^v	ακ
ix. 8	אהה	κ	ακ	ακ
xi. 7	כה	κ	ακ	ακ
8	נאם	κ	ακ	ακ
13	אהה	κ	ακ	ακ
16	כה	κ	ακ	ακ
17	כה	κ	ακ	ακ
21	נאם	κ	ακ	α λεγει κ
xii. 10	כה	κκ	κκ	κκ
19	כה	κ	ακ	ακ
23	כה	κ	ακ	ακ
xii. 25	נאם	κ	ακ	ακ
28a	כה	κ	ακ	ακ
28b	נאם	{om* / κ^amg}	ακ	κ

TABLE IV (*continued*)

MT		B	A	Q
xiii. 3	כה	κ	ακ	ακ
8a	כה	κ	ακ	ακ
8b	נאם	κ	ακ	ακ
9	כי אני	κ	ακ^v	ακ
13	כה	κ	ακ	ακ
16	נאם	κ	ακ	ακ
18	כה	κ	ακ	ακ
20	כה	κκ	κκ	κκ
xiv. 4	כה	κ	ακ	ακ
6	כה	κκ	κκοθ	κκ
11	נאם	κ	{ κ* ακ^a	ακ
14	נאם	κ	{ κ* ακ^a	ακ
16	נאם	κ	{ κ* ακ^a	ακ
18	נאם	κ	{ κ* ακ^a	ακ
20	נאם	κ	{ κ* ακ^a	ακ
21	כה	κ	ακ	ακ
23	נאם	κ	{ κ* ακ^a	ακ
xv. 6	כה	κ	ακ	ακ
8	נאם	κ	κ	ακ
xvi. 3	כה	κ	κ	ακ
8	נאם	κ	{ κ* ακ^a (?)	ακ
14	נאם	κ	{ κ* ακ^a	ακ
19	נאם	κ	κ	ακ
23	נאם	κ	κ	ακ
30	נאם	κ	κ	ακ
36	כה	κ	ακ	ακ
43	נאם	κ	κ	ακ

TABLE IV (*continued*)

MT		B	A	Q
xvi. 48	נאם	κ	κ	ακ
59	כה	κ	ακ	ακ
63	נאם	κ	κ	ακ
xvii. 3	כה	κ	κ	ακ
9	כה	κ	κ	ακ
16	נאם	κ	κ	ακ
19	כה	κ	κ	ακ
22	כה	κ	κ	ακ
xviii. 3	נאם	κ	ακ	ακ
9	נאם	κ	ακ	ακ
23	נאם	κ	κκ	κκ
30	נאם	κ	ακ	ακ
32	נאם	κ	ακ	ακ
xx. 3 a	כה	κ	κ	ακ
3 b	נאם	κ	ακ	ακ
5	כה	κ	κοθ	κοθ
27	כה	κ	$\begin{cases} κ^* \\ ακ^a \end{cases}$	ακ
30	כה	κ	κκοθ	κκ
31	נאם	κ	κ	ακ
33	נאם	$\begin{cases} κ^* \\ κ\ sup\ ras^{ab} \end{cases}$	ακ	ακ
36	נאם	κ	κοθ	κκ
39	כה	κκ	κκ	κκ
40	נאם	κκ	κκ	κκ
44	נאם	κ	ακ	ακ
xxi.3 (xx. 47)	כה	κκ	κοθl	κκ
5 (xx. 49)	אהה	κε κε	κε κε	κε κε
12 (7)	נאם	$\begin{cases} κκ^* \\ κ?\ ^{ab} \end{cases}$	κοθ	κκ
18 (13)	כה	κκ	κκ	$\begin{cases} κκ \\ κ\ πιπι^{mg} \end{cases}$
29 (24)	כה	κ	κκοθ	κκ

TABLE IV (*continued*)

MT		B	A	Q
xxi. 31 (26)	כה	κ	κκοθ	κκ
33 (28)	כה	κ	κοθ	κκ
xxii. 3	כה	κκ	κκοθ	κκ
12	נאם	κ	κκ	κκ
19	כה	κ	κκοθ	κκ
28	כה	κ	κ	ακ
31	נאם	κκ	κκ	κκ
xxiii. 22	כה	κ	κκοθ	κκ
28	כה	κκ	κκοθ	κκ
32	כה	κ	ακκοθ	κκ
34	כה	κ	κκοθ	ακ
35	כה	κ	ακ	ακ
46	כה	κκ	ακ	κκ
49	כי אני	κ	κ	κ
xxiv. 3	כה	κ	ακ	κκ
6	כה	κ	ακ	ακ
9	כה	κ	ακ	ακ
14	נאם	κ	ακ	ακ
21	כה	κ	κκοθ	κκ
24	כי אני	κ	κ	ακ
xxv. 3a	דברי	κυ	κυ	ακ
3b	כה	κ	ακ	ακ
6	כה	κ	κοθ	κκ
8	כה	κ	ακ	ακ
12	כה	κ	ακ	ακ
13	כה	κ	ακ	ακ
14	נאם	κ	κ ras A?	ακ
15	כה	κ	ακ	ακ
16	כה	κ	ακ	ακ
xxvi. 3	כה	κ	ακ	ακ
5	נאם	κ	κκ	ακ
7	כה	κ	ακ	ακ
14	נאם	κ	κ	ακ
15	כה	κκ	ακκ	κκ
19	כה	κκ	κκ	κκ

TABLE IV (*continued*)

MT		B	A	Q
xxvi. 21	נאם	κκ	κοθ	κκ
xxvii. 3	כה	κ	ακκ	κκ
xxviii. 2	כה	κ	κοθ	κκ
6	כה	κ	κκοθ	κκ
10	נאם	κ	ras A?	ακ
12	כה	κκ	κ	κκ
22	כה	κ	ras A?	ακ
24	כי אני	κ	κοθ αυ των	ακ
25	כה	κκ	κκοθ	ακ
3	כה	κ	κοθ	κκ
8	כה	κ	κοθ	κκ
xxix. 13	כה	κ	κκ	κκ
16	כי אני	κ	κοθ	ακ
19	כה	κκ	ακ	κκ
20	נאם	κκ	ακ	κκ
xxx. 2	כה	κ	κ	ακ
6	נאם	κ	κ	ακ
10	כה	κκ	κκ	ακ
13	כה	κκ	κκ	ακ
22	כה	κκ	κκ	κκ
xxxi. 10	כה	κ	ακ	κκ
15	כה	κκ	ακ	κκ
18	נאם	κκ	κκ	κκ
xxxii. 3	כה	κ	ακ	κκ
8	נאם	κκ	κκοθ	κκ
11	כה	{ κ* / κκab	ακ	κκ
14	נאם	κ	ακ	ακ
16	נאם	κκ	κκ	ακ
31	נאם	κκ	κοθ	κκ
32	נאם	κκ	κκοθ	κκ
xxxiii. 11	נאם	κ	{ κ* / ακa sup ras	ακ
25	כה	om	ακ	om
27	כה	κκ	κκ	κκ

TABLE IV (*continued*)

MT		B	A	Q
xxxiv. 2	כה	κκ	κκ	κκ
8	נאם	κκ	κκ	ακ
10	כה	κκ	ακ	κκ
11	כה	{κ* / κκ^{ab}}	κκοθ	κκ
15	כה	κκ	κκ	κκ
17	כה	κκ	κκ	κκ
20	כה	κκ	κκοθ	κκ προς αυτους
30	נאם	{κ* / κκ^{ab}}	κ	κκ
31	נאם	κκ	κκ	κκ
xxxv. 3	כה	κκ	κ	κκ
6	נאם	κκ	κκ	κκ
11	נאם	κ	κκ	κκ
14	כה	κ	κ	κκ
xxxvi. 2	כה	κκ	κκ	κκ
3	כה	κκ	κκοθ	κκ
4a	דברי	κυ	κυ	ακυ
4b	כה	κ	κ	κκ
5	כה	κκ	κ	κκ
6	כה	κ	ακ	κκ
7	כה	om	om	*ακ
13	כה	κκ	ακ	κκ
14	נאם	κκ	ακ	κκ
15	נאם	κκ	κκοθ	κκ
22	כה	κ	ακ	κκ
23	נאם	κ	λεγ. ακ	{*λεγ ακ / α πιπι^{mg}}
32	נאם	{κκ* / ακ^{abmg}}	κκοθ	κκ
33	כה	ακ	κοθ	κκ
37	כה	ακ	κκοθ	κκ
xxxvii. 3	וְאָמַר	κε	κε κε	κε κε
5	כה	κ	κκ	κκ
9	כה	κ	κκ	κκ

TABLE IV (*continued*)

MT		B	A	Q
xxxvii. 12	כה	κ	ακ	κκ
19	כה	κ	ακ	κκ
21	כה	κκ	ακοθ	κκ
xxxviii. 3	כה	κκ	ακ	κκ
10	כה	κκ	κκοθ	κκ
14	כה	κ	κκοθ	κκ
17	כה	κκ	ακοθ	κκ
18	נאם	κκ	κκοθ	κκ
21	נאם	κ	κκ	κκ
xxxix. 1	כה	κ	κκ	κκ
5	נאם	κ	κκ	κκ
8	נאם	κκ	κκοθ	κκ
10	נאם	κ	κ	κκ
13	נאם	κ	κ	κκ
17	כה	κ	κ	κκ
20	נאם	κ	κκ	κκ
25	כה	κκ	κκοθ	κκ
29	נאם	κκ	κκ	κκ
xliii. 18	כה	κοθl	κοθl	κκ
19	נאם	κοθ	κοθ	κκ
27	נאם	κ	κ	κκ
xliv. 6	כה	κοθ	κοθ	κκ
9	כה	κοθ	κοθ	κοθ
12	נאם	κοθ	κοθ	κοθ
15	נאם	κοθ	κοθ	κοθ
27	נאם	κοθ	κοθ	κοθ
xlv. 9a	כה	κθ	κοθ	κκ
9b	נאם	κ̇θ	κοθ	κοθ
15	נאם	κθ	κοθ	κοθ
18	כה	κθ	κοθ	κοθ
xlvi. 1	כה	κθ	κοθ	κοθ
16	כה	κθ	ακ	κοθ
xlvii. 13	כה	κθ	κοθ	κοθ
23	נאם	κθ	κοθ	κοθ
xlviii. 29	נאם	κθ	κοθ	κοθ

TABLE V

LXX renderings of אדני יהוה in Ezekiel

(Shewing differences between chapters i–xx (or xxvii),
xxi (or xxviii)–xxxix, xl–xlviii)

	i–xx 78 אדני יהוה			xxi–xxxix 122 ’י ’א			xl–xlviii 17 ’י ’א		
	B	A	Q	B	A	Q	B	A	Q
κύριος	72	16	1	68	21	1	1	1	0
ἀδωναὶ κύριος	0	49	66	2	33	31	0	1	0
κύριος κύριος	5	11	10	49	52	89	0	0	5
κύριος ὁ θεός	1	2	1	0	15	0	16	15	12
Omit	0	0	0	3	1	1	0	0	0
	78	78	78	122	122	122	17	17	17

or

	i–xxvii 120 ’י ’א			xxviii–xxxix 80 ’י ’א		
	B	A	Q	B	A	Q
κύριος	103	22	2	37	15	0
ἀδωναὶ κύριος	0	63	84	2	19	13
κύριος κύριος	16	29	33	38	34	66
κύριος ὁ θεός	1	6	1	0	11	0
Omit	0	0	0	3	1	1
	120	120	120	80	80	80

Table VI

κύριος κύριος in chapters i–xxxix

MT		B	A	Q
xii. 10	כה	κκ	κκ	κκ
xiii. 20	כה	κκ	κκ	κκ
xiv. 6	כה	κκ	κκοθ	κκ
xx. 39	כה	κκ	κκ	κκ
40	נאם	κκ	κκ (after Ἰσραήλ)	κκ
xx. 47 (= xxi. 3)	כה	κκ	κοθ	κκ
49 (= xxi. 5)	אהה	κκ	κκ	κκ
xxi. 7 (= 12)	נאם	{κκ / κ?ab}	κοθ	κκ
13 (= 18)	כה	κκ	κκ	κκ
xxii. 3	כה	κκ	κοθ	κκ
31	נאם	κκ	κκ	κκ
xxiii. 28	כה	κκ	κκοθ	κκ
46	כה	κκ	ακ^v	κκ
xxvi. 15	כה	κκ	ακκ	κκ
19	כה	κκ	κκ	κκ
21	נאם	κκ	κκοθ	κκ
xxviii. 12	כה	κκ	κ	κκ
25	כה	κκ	κκοθ	ακ^v
xxix. 19	כה	κκ	ακ^v	κκ
20	נאם	κκ	ακ^v	κκ
xxx. 10	כה	κκ	ακ^v	κκ
13	כה	κκ	ακ	κκ
22	כה	κκ	κκ	κκ
xxxi. 15	כה	κκ	ακ^v	κκ
18	נאם	κκ	κκ	κκ
xxxii. 8	נאם	κκ	κκοθ	κκ
[11	כה	{κ* / κκ^ab}	ακ	κκ]
16	נאם	κκ	κκ	κκ
31	נאם	κκ	κοθ	κκ

TABLE VI (*continued*)

MT		B	A	Q
xxxii. 32	נאם	κκ	κκοθ	κκ
xxxiii. 27	כה	κκ	κκ	κκ
xxxiv. 2	כה	κκ	κκ	κκ
8	נאם	κκ	κκ	ακ
10	כה	κκ	ακ	κκ
[11	כה	{κ* / κκ^{ab}}	κκοθ	κκ]
15	כה	κκ	κκ	κκ
17	כה	κκ	κκ	κκ
20	כה	κκ	κκοθ	κκ πρ αὐτ
[30	נאם	{κ* / κκ^{ab}}	κ	κκ]
31	נאם	κκ	κκ	κκ
xxxv. 3	כה	κκ	κ	κκ
6	נאם	κκ	κκ	κκ
xxxvi. 2	כה	κκ	κκ	κκ
3	כה	κκ	κκοθ	κκ
5	כה	κκ	κ	κκ
13	כה	κκ	ακ	κκ
14	נאם	κκ	ακ	κκ
15	נאם	κκ	κοθ	κκ
32	נאם	κκ	κκοθ	κκ
xxxvii. 21	כה	κκ	ακοθ	κκ
xxxviii. 3	כה	κκ	ακ^v	κκ
10	כה	κκ	κκοθ	κκ
17	כה	κκ	ακοθ	κκ
18	נאם	κκ	κκοθ	κκ
xxxix. 8	נאם	κκ	κκοθ	κκ
25	כה	κκ	κκοθ	κκ
29	נאם	κκ	κκ	κκ

In this table in addition to the 54 κκ in B, we find three more in B^{ab} (xxxii. 11, xxxiv. 11, 30) and in xxxvi. 33, 37 we have two ακ in B (where A has κοθ in one and κκοθ in the other, and Q has in both cases κκ). A has 20 κκ (+ 1 in xxxvi. 37), 14 κκοθ (+ 1 in xxxvi. 37), 5 κοθ (+ 1 in xxxvi. 33), 11 ακ (+ 1 ακκ, 2 ακοθ) and 4 κ alone. Q has κκ in these passages 52 times and ακ twice (xxviii. 25, xxxiv. 8).

INDEX

For EU product safety concerns, contact us at Calle de José Abascal, 56–1°, 28003 Madrid, Spain or eugpsr@cambridge.org.

www.ingramcontent.com/pod-product-compliance
Ingram Content Group UK Ltd.
Pitfield, Milton Keynes, MK11 3LW, UK
UKHW012332130625
459647UK00009B/228